MUSIC LICENSING:
A PRACTICAL GUIDE

This Guide is not intended to be a legal treatise or to convey legal advice. It is intended only to provide a basic understanding of music licensing in broadcast and related industries.

Please consult an attorney if you need help with specific issues relating to music use licensing.

Second Edition

Copyright © 2024 by Television Music License Committee LLC

All rights reserved. No part of this publication may be reproduced, stored or transmitted in any form or by any means, electronic, mechanical, photocopying, recording, scanning, or otherwise without written permission from the publisher. It is illegal to copy this book, post it to a website, or distribute it by any other means without permission, except in the case of brief quotations embodied in critical reviews and certain other noncommercial uses permitted by copyright law.

Printed in the United States.

ISBN: 978-1-7377708-3-1 paperback
ISBN: 978-1-7377708-2-4 ebook

MUSIC LICENSING:
A PRACTICAL GUIDE

(FOR BROADCASTERS AND OTHER MUSIC LICENSEES)

JANET E. McHUGH

A NOTE ABOUT THE AUTHOR

Janet E. McHugh is a seasoned corporate executive and attorney with experience in the energy, finance, and broadcast industries. She has been President and CEO of the Television Music License Committee (TVMLC) since 2016.

Prior to TVMLC, she was an attorney with Sinclair Broadcast Group, Inc. where she handled and managed operational legal matters including the negotiation of commercial contracts, insurance, real estate, and music licensing. Prior to Sinclair, Janet served as Deputy General Counsel and Senior Vice President of Human Resources for Constellation Energy Group, Inc., now Exelon Corp.

Janet is a graduate of Clemson University and Duke University School of Law. As a public service, Janet chaired and served on the Maryland State Ethics Commission for many years. Janet has two children: a son who graduated from Duke University and is a patent litigator in New York and a daughter who graduated from Clemson University and has been a local broadcasting host and reporter since 2015.

Janet's contact email is janet@tvmlc.com.

DEDICATION

This Guide is dedicated to local TV station employees—those folks who constantly work under tight deadlines, often with limited budgets. It's for the business managers, accountants, in-house counsel, and all of those assisting them who are, from time to time, asked to add music licensing to their already full plates.

This Guide is also dedicated to the members of the Television Music License Committee who volunteer their time to keep music performance license fees reasonable, benefiting and protecting local TV stations — with special recognition and appreciation of Doug Lowe, Jim MacDermott and David Amy who contributed their time and talents to the Committee for decades.

Finally, this book is dedicated to my daughter, Ellen Meny and many other on-air broadcasters. They have dedicated themselves to informing and entertaining millions of local TV station viewers from Yakima, Washington to Washington D.C. Our local TV and radio stations are the journalistic heart of our communities. "Live long and prosper."

TABLE OF CONTENTS

Introduction i

Section 1 An Introduction to Copyright Law 1

Section 2 Digging Deeper:
Music Licensing and the Law 9

Section 3 The Music Business 15

Section 4 Licensing Terminology 21

Section 5 The Players 29

Section 6 Musical Works:
Public Performance Rights–General 45

Section 7 Musical Works:
Public Performance Rights—Broadcast Radio 51

Section 8 Musical Works: Public Performance
Rights—Broadcast TV 59

Section 9 PRO Market Share 71

Section 10 Sound Recordings 73

Section 11 Reproduction and Distribution Licenses 83

Section 12 Synchronization Rights 91

Section 13 Judicial and Legislative History 97

Section 14 The Consent Decrees 103

Section 15 Fair Use and Related Topics 113

Section 16 "Hot" Issues 119

Section 17 The Future: Creation of a Public,
Universal Database 125

Afterword 133

Additional reading – Fair Use – Section 15 135

Resources 137

INTRODUCTION

As an attorney working for a large U.S. broadcast company, I was assigned projects related to music licensing that took me down some deep rabbit holes - searching for answers to questions that could significantly impact the bottom line. Accountants and business managers working at local TV stations would ask me to help them figure out the fees that the station owed performance rights organizations (PROs) like ASCAP and BMI. Local news producers wanted to know if they could use a Taylor Swift song in a segment or broadcast their local July 4th fireworks show (timed to music) without running afoul of the copyright laws.

So many questions—and the answers weren't easy to find. I called the Television Music License Committee (TVMLC) regularly and got the help I needed. But I still didn't really understand music licensing. When I became President and CEO of the Committee, I began to focus on communication and education. I wanted to make music licensing understandable to those folks who only focus on this area of the business occasionally.

There are billions of dollars associated with music licensing. For several years, ASCAP and BMI have both reported record-breaking annual revenues of over $1 billion. This includes hundreds of millions of dollars from local broadcasters—even in a pandemic year. ASCAP and BMI are just two of the organizations that collect fees from the broadcast industry and pay royalties to songwriters, composers, and music publishers. There are more.

While the fees paid to music providers are a substantial part of broadcast company budgets, employees of many TV stations don't understand how music licensing fees are calculated, who receives the money, and why those fees need to be paid. This Guide will answer these questions and provide a general overview of music use licensing with a particular focus on local radio and TV broadcasting.

What follows is not intended as a comprehensive analysis of music and copyright law; instead, it is designed to provide a practical look at what can be a very complex and misunderstood area of the law. It is primarily a guide for lawyers and non-lawyers who find themselves—even tangentially—working on matters relating to music licensing.

This Guide is meant to be a resource. You don't need to read it sequentially. You can read the sections that help you now and skip those that don't. Frequently asked questions are scattered through the Guide under the heading: "**QUESTIONS FROM OUR AUDIENCE.**" There will be periodic updates to this Guide. We encourage your feedback.

SECTION 1

AN INTRODUCTION TO COPYRIGHT LAW

Rules governing the rights of copyright holders are extensive. Here is an entry point with information that can lead you into a more nuanced understanding when you read later chapters.

THE BASICS

Any discussion of music licensing must begin with the United States copyright law (copyright law), which bestows certain rights upon artists and creators of musical compositions. If you are not familiar with copyright law and need to understand music licensing, do not worry. Here are some basics, starting with what is protected by copyright law and what is not.

The primary purpose of copyright law is to promote creative expression. The law allows creators or "authors" of literary, musical, and other forms of expression to control, for a period of years, how their works are used—that is, how they are reproduced, distributed, and performed.

The theory of copyright is that the public is served by fairly compensating artists for their work. Fair compensation encourages the creation and wide distribution of original works, filling the world with all manner of entertainment, such as music, literature, and film.

Copyright law protects many types of expression but does not protect ideas. Only embodiments of ideas in "tangible" forms of expression—

such as a book, recorded music, or a film—are protected. While the idea of star-crossed lovers is an interesting topic, it is not exclusive to anyone. But literary or film works incorporating the idea—Shakespeare's "Romeo and Juliet" or the films "Titanic" and "West Side Story"—are protectable by copyright law.

> Copyright law protects many types of expression but does not protect ideas. Only embodiments of ideas in "tangible" forms of expression—such as a book, recorded music, or a film—are protected.

The work involved must possess sufficient creativity to warrant copyright protection. While this is not a high standard, copyright law does not, for example, protect most song titles alone (as opposed to song lyrics or the music itself). That's because song titles comprising only a few words do not have sufficient creative content.

Copyright law provides the creator or owner of a written, musical, or other work certain exclusive rights. In broadcast terms, a company must obtain clearance before using a copyrighted work created and/or owned by another person.

The creator/owner of the work typically has several fundamental rights for a period of years. They can:

1. Reproduce the copyrighted work in copies or phonorecords;
2. Prepare derivative works based upon the copyrighted work;
3. Distribute copies or phonorecords of the copyrighted work to the public by sale or other transfer of ownership, or by rental, lease, or lending;
4. Perform the copyrighted work publicly in the case of literary, musical, dramatic, choreographic works, pantomimes, motion pictures, and other audiovisual works;
5. Display the copyrighted work publicly in the case of literary, musical, dramatic, and choreographic works, pantomimes, as

well as pictorial, graphic, or sculptural works—including the individual images of a motion picture or other audiovisual work;

6. Perform the copyrighted work publicly using a digital audio transmission in the case of sound recordings.

Without a proper license from a creator or owner, no one else has the right to take any of these actions. Unless such permission is granted (or an exception applies), the copying, public distribution, public performance, public display, or creation of so-called "derivative" works are generally prohibited. Violators are subject to monetary and other penalties.

While there will be further details about all the rights listed above, performance rights are among the most important to broadcasters. Because of that, this Guide devotes considerable time to those rights and how they are licensed to broadcasters.

One of a copyright owner's broadest rights is the right of that owner to create a derivative work, or a work based on already existing pieces of creative content. Common derivative works include translations, musical arrangements, motion picture versions of literary material or plays, art reproductions, abridgments, and condensations of preexisting material.

The type of derivative work that's perhaps most well-known is an author's right to adapt a book into a screenplay. They can turn that book into a Broadway show or a movie. Think "To Kill a Mockingbird," "The Color Purple," and of course, "The Harry Potter" franchise.

Copyright law vests the original work's copyright owner with the exclusive right to prepare derivative works. Therefore, the owner of the preexisting work must authorize the creation of a derivative work for it to be non-infringing. The most common means of securing permission is through a license covering particular uses for a specified period.

A rightsholder can sell the copyright outright in whole or transfer only a subset of certain rights. This is similar to renting your house for a limited time and under certain conditions. For example, J.K. Rowling can grant permission to a producer to adapt some of her books into a series of movies without losing the right to sell her books exclusively. Creators of music can grant Netflix permission to use their music in a produced show. But the creators can still license the right to perform that same music to an event producer for a live concert.

Rights granted by the copyright laws can be co-owned. And a work that is collaboratively created, for example, by a composer and a lyricist, or by two lyricists, is considered a "joint work." Think about famous collaborators such as Elton John and Bernie Taupin. Co-authors of a joint work are co-owners of the copyright. Under the copyright law's default rule, any one co-owner is free to license the entire work on a non-exclusive basis, even without the participation of the other co-owners. The licensing co-owner then has the duty to share the resulting royalties with the other co-owners.

Now that you have a general overview, let's dig into more specifics.

PRIMARY RESOURCES

Any discussion must begin with the U.S. Copyright Office. That arm of the U.S. government administers the national copyright system and provides advice on copyright law to Congress, federal agencies, the courts, and the public. Its website, www.copyright.gov, provides useful links to various aspects of the law and the operation of the office itself.

Another resource is the "United States Code"—the country's official compilation and codification of general and permanent federal statutes. You can find relevant information on copyright law in Title 17, sections 1-8 and 10-12.

The Copyright Act of 1976 thoroughly revised Title 17. The Act provides the basic framework for current copyright law and was enacted on Oct. 19, 1976 (Pub. L. No. 94-553, 90 Stat. 2541).

> **THE U.S. COPYRIGHT OFFICE'S WEBSITE ALSO HAS SEVERAL FAQS. HERE, VERBATIM, ARE SOME OF THE MOST IMPORTANT ONES:**
>
> **What does copyright protect?**
> Copyright, a form of intellectual property law, protects original works of authorship including literary, dramatic, musical, and artistic works, such as poetry, novels, movies, songs, computer software, and architecture. Copyright does not protect facts, ideas, systems, or methods of operation, although it may protect the way these things are expressed.
>
> **How is a copyright different from a patent or a trademark?**
> Copyright protects original works of authorship, while a patent protects inventions or discoveries. Ideas and discoveries are not protected by the copyright law, although the way in which they are expressed may be. A trademark protects words, phrases, symbols, or designs identifying the source of the goods or services of one party and distinguishing them from those of others.
>
> **When is my work protected?**
> Your work is under copyright protection the moment it is created and fixed in a tangible form that it is perceptible either directly or with the aid of a machine or device.
>
> **Do I have to register with your office to be protected?**
> No. In general, registration is voluntary. Copyright exists from the moment the work is created. You will have to register, however, if you wish to bring a lawsuit for infringement of a U.S. work.

The last question from the Copyright Office on the side bar is critical for music licensing. Because books, musical works, and other copyrightable materials are not required to be registered with the U.S. Copyright

Office, there is no official comprehensive database of registered works. There is no one place that we can find a list of all musical works created. This becomes important as you learn more about music licensing in this Guide.

CRITICAL INFORMATION

Duration—One critical question concerns how long an owner legally possesses their rights. The answer depends on when the work was created.

Works created after January 1, 1978, are protected from the time they first take fixed, tangible form until the end of the creator's life and then generally lasts an additional 70 years after their death. In the case of a joint work with more than one author, the term of protection generally lasts 70 years after the last surviving author's death.

If the work is a "work made for hire," i.e., a work made by an employee within the scope of their employment or certain limited types of works created by independent contractors who were specially commissioned to create the works on a work made for hire basis, then the employer or commissioning party is treated as the author of the work. The duration of copyright protection for a work made for hire is 95 years from the date the work was first published or 120 years from the date of creation, whichever comes first. That's according to the Copyright Act of 1976, as amended by the Sonny Bono Copyright Term Extension Act of 1998.

The copyright duration for works created before 1978 will vary depending on several factors. These are outlined in 17 U.S.C. Sec. 303.

PENALTIES

When copyright violations occur, the penalties can be significant—whether or not you intended to violate the law. In simple terms, if you violate the copyright laws, the following can happen:

- An infringer can be ordered to pay the actual dollar amount of harm to the copyright owner and/or turn over any profits earned by the violator as a result of the infringement.

- Alternatively, the copyright owner can elect to be awarded statutory damages, ranging from $750 to $30,000 for each work infringed. In the case of willful infringement, it can be increased to as much as $150,000 for each work infringed. Statutory damages are the most common form of damages sought.

- If the dispute goes to trial and copyright infringement is found, the losing infringer can be ordered to pay the copyright owner's reasonable attorney fees and certain costs.

- A court can stop infringement by issuing an injunction.

- A court can take control of the infringing works.

- An infringer can go to jail for especially egregious infringing acts.

For more information and the statutory language, see www.copyright.gov/title17/92chap5.html.

SECTION 2

DIGGING DEEPER: MUSIC LICENSING AND THE LAW

Now that you have a basic understanding of copyright law, let's summarize how the copyright laws protect music creators in particular.

Certain essential concepts will help make things clear. First and foremost, you need to understand the difference between musical works and sound recordings.

A musical work refers to a songwriter's musical composition and lyrics.

A sound recording is a particular version of a musician singing and/or playing a musical work that is captured or "fixed" in a recording medium (vinyl records, CDs, or digital files).

RIGHTS GIVEN TO MUSIC CREATORS UNDER THE COPYRIGHT LAWS

Songwriters, composers, and recording artists have several exclusive rights under copyright laws.

As noted in the previous section, owners of musical works have specific distribution and reproduction rights: they can copy and distribute their works as they see fit.

The most lucrative right of ownership that the owners of musical works

> **A musical work** refers to a songwriter's musical composition and lyrics.
>
> **A sound recording** is a particular version of a musician singing and/or playing a musical work that is captured or "fixed" in a recording medium (vinyl records, CDs, or digital files).
>
> **Performance rights** refers to the exclusive power or privilege to either perform a musical work or authorize others to perform the musical work publicly.
>
> **Synchronization rights** are required when music is combined with audiovisual content, taking the form of a film or TV program.

possess is the right of the owner to "publicly perform" the musical work. Some estimate that revenue from public performances of musical works constitute 50% of music publishing revenue.

The copyright law entitles the owners of musical compositions to compensation when their works are "publicly performed." Laws and the courts continue to define precisely what that term means.

Under 17 U.S.C. Sec. 101, to perform means to "recite, render, [or] play..., either directly or by means of a device or process...." An entertainer performs music live in stadiums and concert halls. Local radio stations perform music through broadcast transmission to listeners. A TV broadcaster performs music when it transmits a program to its audience.

Performance rights refers to the exclusive power or privilege to either perform a musical work or authorize others to perform the musical work publicly, according to 17 U.S.C. Sec. 106 (4). It does not matter whether the performance is for profit or not (although that can impact the license fee).

Synchronization rights are required when music is combined with audiovisual content, taking the form of a film or TV program. See Section 12. When a TV producer captures video highlights from a local high school football game and times the video to music for a local news sports segment, that is a synchronization.

According to the Copyright Office, "the synchronization (or 'synch' right) is a species of the reproduction right." However, it also includes the right to prepare a derivative work and, in some instances, may include public distribution rights if the resulting audiovisual work will be distributed in copies, such as DVDs, Blu-Rays, or downloads.

Films and TV shows can require clearance of both public performance rights and synchronization rights. Both rights must be obtained before the content is presented publicly, whether on the "big screen" or "small screen."

> Broadcasters generally acquire performance rights under their licenses with performance rights organizations (PROs). Synchronization rights are usually obtained by program producers in direct negotiations with the composer or music publisher.

While the rightsholders in musical works have the rights summarized above, rightsholders in sound recordings are given separate rights under the copyright laws.

In 1973, Dolly Parton wrote and recorded her version of the song "I Will Always Love You." For the 1992 film "The Bodyguard," the same song was recorded by Whitney Houston.

Parton and her publisher owned the rights to the musical work. However, Parton and Houston (or their respective record labels) each owned the sound recording rights to the version of the musical work they recorded.

The owners of sound recordings have various rights under the copyright laws, including the right to make and distribute copies of the recording in either physical or digital forms. These rights are known as reproduction and distribution rights.

In 1995, Congress gave sound recording owners an exclusive public performance right. However, it's limited to digital audio transmissions.

In recent years this has become a significant source of revenue for owners of sound recordings as listeners consume more music through Spotify and other digital audio services.

Traditional over-the-air broadcasters, particularly local radio, were expressly exempted from having to secure sound recording performance rights. In other words, Spotify pays artists like Parton or Houston for the performance of their sound recordings, but local radio does not. Local over-the-air radio, however, does pay for the performance of musical works. In other words, these radio stations pay for Parton's songwriting but not for Houston's or Parton's recordings.

Both the owners of musical works and the owners of sound recordings have reproduction rights that will be discussed in detail in Sections 10 and 11.

TRANSFERRING RIGHTS: LICENSES

The rights described above are exclusive to the copyright owner (or if the owner has transferred his/her rights – the rightsholder). When the owner or holder extends their rights to others, they can dictate the terms.

At a high level of generality, it's no different from owning real estate property. If you own a building and rent your property out to others, the renters must agree to your terms. If someone occupies your property without permission, you can take legal action against them. Copyright is no different.

Copyright owners have an exclusive claim of ownership. When they grant permission for someone to broadcast their work on the radio, the broadcaster does not own that work. They only have the right to perform that music under the terms agreed to with the copyright owner.

Generally, a person "infringes" upon the copyright of another when they fail to get or receive the owner's permission to use the copyrighted work. As recourse, the copyright owner can sue the infringer and collect damages.

A license is a legal agreement that gives certain companies or individuals permission to use copyrighted music. A license generally is limited to specific terms and scope dictating how long the music can be used, the ways it can be used, and how much the user must pay.

As you will read in subsequent sections of this Guide, some licenses are created in private, commercial transactions negotiated in the open market. In other cases, government regulations can impact licensing.

> A license is a legal agreement that gives certain companies or individuals permission to use copyrighted music.

POINTS TO REMEMBER

- U.S. Copyright laws give music creators and recording artists certain rights and protect them against certain uses of their music without their permission. Use of copyrighted music without obtaining permission from the rightsholders of that music generally is a violation of law (unless an exception applies). Permission is typically granted through licenses.
- A musical work refers to a songwriter's musical composition and lyrics.
- A sound recording is a particular version of a musician singing and/or playing a musical work that is captured or "fixed" in a recording medium.
- The owners of musical works have the following protected rights—

Musical works performance rights refer to the right of a creator of a musical work to publicly perform a composition whether live or via broadcast or digital transmission.
  - Broadcasters generally acquire musical works performance rights from PROs.

Synchronization rights are required when music is combined with audiovisual content.
  - Broadcasters typically get synch rights directly from publishers or music libraries.

- Films and TV shows typically require clearance of both public performance rights and synchronization rights.
- Both the owners of musical works and the owners of sound recordings have reproductions rights.
- Sound recording public performance right is limited to digital audio transmissions (over-the-air broadcasters need not secure sound recording performance rights).

SECTION 3

THE MUSIC BUSINESS

While understanding the law underlying music licensing is important, it also helps to "follow the money."

No discussion of music licensing is complete without a short description of the music business—or how your favorite artist or composer gets paid. More information on this topic can be found in Section 5, titled "The Players."

First, here are a few definitions:

MUSICAL WORKS

Composers or songwriters write music and/or lyrics (they create "musical works").

Publishers are assigned rights to the musical works by composers and songwriters. The largest music publishers include Universal Music Publishing Group, Sony/ATV Music Publishing, and Warner/Chappell (the Big Three).

Publishers work with and represent composers and songwriters.

Musical Work is the songwriter or composer's underlying musical composition along with any accompanying lyrics. **Songwriters and composers are the creators of musical works,** and they have different rights than those who perform their musical works.

SOUND RECORDINGS

Artists perform and record the "musical work." Think Nikki Minaj or Lizzo who create "sound recordings."

Record companies provide marketing and administrative services to the artists. Yes, they are still called "record" companies. The parent companies that own the Big Three also have record company divisions—Universal Music Group, Sony Music Entertainment, Inc. and Warner Music Group.

Record companies or "labels" work with and represent sound recording artists.

FOLLOW THE MONEY

Money flows directly from certain music users like Spotify back to artists through record companies. However, there is often a two-step process for payments to composers, songwriters, and publishers. TV, radio, streaming services, and other music users pay performance rights organizations (PROs), such as ASCAP, BMI, and SESAC. The PROs, in turn, pay publishers, composers, and songwriters.

Who are the record companies and publishers, and how does everyone make money? As mentioned above, the parent companies of the three major publishers also have record label divisions. A substantial amount of money that flows from consumers to artists and composers goes through these large corporations.

In other words, royalties paid to composers and songwriters for musical works and royalties paid to recording artists for sound recordings often end up in the same corporate pocket. All these publishers and record labels have relationships with famous and legendary artists such as Lady Gaga (Universal), Bruce Springsteen and Barbara Streisand (Sony), and Madonna (Warner), to name just a few.

You can bet that if an artist is a household name, they are affiliated with one of the Big Three. There are still many independent record labels, and some do represent famous artists, but independent record labels often get acquired by one of the Big Three.

> The three major publishers generated more than $3.2 billion in 2019 or $369,000 per hour, according to a dramatic headline in Rolling Stone, published March 2, 2020. When you combine these revenues with those earned by the Big Three record labels, the total earned is more than $18 billion.

Not surprisingly, more money flows to the major record labels than the major music publishers. According to Rolling Stone, "Generally speaking, the owners of the rights to the written song (repped by a publisher) are paid approximately a fifth of the amount of money paid to artists (and the labels repping them) for the performance of the same track on Spotify."

For every dollar received for the use of a musical work or sound recording, the publisher or record label keep a significant portion for themselves. This amount is to compensate the companies—generously, I would say—for various activities. They include promoting an artist's latest song to get radio airplay; royalty collection from music users; negotiation of licenses; and other "back office" services. In many cases, music publishing income from licensing a creator's rights is divided 50/50 between the creator and publisher.

Once a composer cuts a deal with a publisher, they frequently lose control over how their compositions are used and distributed. As both a songwriter and recording artist, Taylor Swift lost control of her early works to a publishing company.

Some artists—including Bob Dylan, Bruce Springsteen, and Neil Diamond—kept their publishing rights to maintain complete control over their compositions. Recently, Dylan sold his entire catalog and all his rights in that catalog to Universal Music for an undisclosed amount. It was rumored to be $300 million, which would make it the largest acquisition of a single act's publishing rights. Dylan is 79 years old, as of this writing, and he had long controlled the vast majority of his songwriting copyrights. For years, he aggressively marketed his music and even licensed his compositions for use in television commercials. With Universal in charge, Dylan likely no longer has veto power over how his songs are used.

Interestingly, the deal only covers existing works. If Dylan chooses to write songs as an octogenarian, he'll likely retain control of the new works' usage. Stevie Nicks did a similar deal (rumored to be $80 million) with a lesser-known publisher.

Music is big business, with substantial amounts of money flowing from music users to rightsholders. The remainder of this Guide will help you understand the legal underpinnings of the music business and how the law impacts the flow of money.

FLOW OF MONEY

MUSICAL WORKS

Music Users

↓ License Fees

PROs

↓ Royalties

Music Publishers

↑ Music Rights

Composers/Songwriters

SOUND RECORDINGS

Music Users

↓ License Fees

Record Labels

↓ Royalties ↑ Music Rights

Recording Artists

SECTION 4

LICENSING TERMINOLOGY

There's a "secret sauce" to understanding music licensing: knowing the terminology and the players.

Music users need to understand some essential terms when they acquire licensing rights. They can be complex and are often confusing. Here are some of the most frequently used and least understood concepts.

THE BASICS

Musical Work is the songwriter or composer's underlying musical composition along with any accompanying lyrics. **Songwriters and composers are the creators of musical works,** and they have different rights than those who perform their musical works.

Rightsholders in musical works have the following exclusive rights and can prevent others from exercising these rights:

- *Reproduction* of the copyrighted musical work;
- *Preparation* of derivative works based on the copyrighted musical work;
- *Distribution* of the musical work to the public by sale, rental, lease, or lending;
- *Performance* of the musical work publicly;
- *Display* (or show a copy) of the musical work publicly.

Sound Recording is the recorded version of a musician singing or playing a unique rendition of an underlying musical work. It is the particular performance of a musical work fixed in a recording medium such as a CD or digital file. Sound recordings can be created by one person or a group of musicians–such as lead singers, an orchestra, or backup singers. **Performing artists and their record labels produce sound recordings** by recording a particular performance of a musical work (frequently in a recording studio).

> **Sound Recording** is the recorded version of a musician singing or playing a unique rendition of an underlying musical work.

People who hold the exclusive rights to sound recordings control the ability of others to:

- *Reproduce* the copyrighted sound recording;
- *Prepare* derivative works based on the copyrighted sound recording;
- *Distribute* phonorecords (such as CDs, MP3s or other digital files, vinyl, etc.) of the sound recording to the public by sale, rental, lease, or lending;
- *Publicly perform the sound recording by means of a digital audio transmission.*

LICENSING

License is the permission to use another person's property for a specific time period and under specified conditions. It usually requires payment for the use of the property. Bruce Springsteen does not give his music away for free!

Royalties are fees paid to a rightsholder, such as a songwriter or publisher for a musical work and the artist or record label for a sound recording. Taylor Swift gets royalties for the songs she composes and records. The heirs of a deceased artist such as Frank Sinatra get royalties for the songs he recorded (but he never composed any of those songs).

Performing artists and their record labels produce sound recordings by recording a particular performance of a musical work (frequently in a recording studio).

Blanket License, as it pertains to musical works public performances, is the right to publicly perform all the works in the repertory of a publisher or performance rights organization (PRO).

Per Program License is a term most relevant to musical works licensing by TV broadcasters and is the right to publicly perform all the works in the repertory of a PRO with a fee that varies depending on use and whether musical works are licensed directly from the copyright holder or through a PRO. More about per program licenses can be found in Section 8.

Direct License is a license that is entered between the rightsholder and the music user without the assistance of an intermediary such as a PRO. All members and affiliates of ASCAP and BMI have the right to directly negotiate non-exclusive licenses with music users, such as TV and radio stations. In other words, a composer or songwriter can cut deals with media outlets, bypassing ASCAP or BMI. In broadcast TV, music libraries often provide direct licenses. The ASCAP and BMI consent decrees prohibit those PROs from preventing their members and affiliates from entering into direct licenses. These decrees are described in Section 14 of this Guide.

Source Licenses are obtained from composers, songwriters, and/or publishers (the rightsholders) of particular music by program producers. The program producers can then pass on the right to use music under these "licenses from the source" to media outlets airing the producer's programs.

Statutory License is a license that a copyright owner is compelled to give without a voluntary, private, negotiated commercial transaction. Copyright laws dictate which types of music users are eligible for these licenses and the rates and terms are generally set by the Copyright Royalty Board (CRB). They are sometimes referred to as "compulsory licenses." As noted later in this Guide, statutory licenses are covered by Sections 112, 114, and 115 of the U.S. Copyright Act. For example, Sirius XM can secure all the sound recording rights it needs for its satellite radio service through a statutory license. Similarly, radio broadcasters that simulcast their programming over the internet can secure the necessary sound recording rights through a statutory license.

PERFORMANCE RIGHTS VS. SYNCHRONIZATION RIGHTS

The difference between performance and synchronization rights is a critical concept that broadcasters need to know. Both types of rights can be needed before TV shows, films, or other types of audiovisual content are made available to the public.

Synchronization (often shortened to "synch") refers to the use of music in "timed-relation" to visual content. Think of it as "synching" music to video content or the simple production of content with music. These licenses typically cover the right to prepare a derivative work (by incorporating pre-existing music into a new audiovisual work), the duplication right, and sometimes the public distribution right. By industry custom, synch licenses do not typically include public performance rights.

Performance refers to the exclusive right of copyright owners to publicly perform their works. We will devote several chapters of this Guide to public performance rights and how the music users pay PROs for the right to perform composers' and songwriters' musical works in public.

> For our TV broadcasters, think of it this way –
>
> For the musical work (i.e., the underlying composition), you need synchronization rights to "use" the music in any video production. You need performance rights to broadcast whatever is produced using music – TV segment, program, or other audiovisual content.

If you produce content using a pre-existing sound recording including popular music, you need to obtain a master use license.

Clearance of all the above is typically required before pre-recorded audiovisual content using music can be transmitted to the public.

See Section 12 for more information about synchronization rights.

DIGITAL MUSIC

Interactive Service refers to companies that provide music on demand, such as Spotify or Apple Music, where the listener can make individual selection of listening choices in what is sometimes known as a "lean forward" experience. As defined by 17 U.S.C. Sec. 114 (j) (7) of the Copyright Act, "an 'interactive service' is one that enables a member of the public to receive a transmission of a program specially created for the recipient, or on request, a transmission of a particular sound recording, whether or not as part of a program, which is selected by or on behalf of the recipient."

Noninteractive Service refers to companies like Pandora's flagship ad-supported service and the ad-supported version of iHeart Radio's digital streaming service. Services that engage in simulcast streaming of over-the-air radio broadcasts are also considered noninteractive services. Section 114 of the Copyright Act categorizes several types of services as noninteractive. Generally, they do not allow a listener, user, or subscriber to select specific recordings on-demand. Instead, they provide a "lean back" experience.

Digital services are the fastest growing means of music consumption. You can find out more about their licensing requirements in Sections 10 and 11 of this Guide.

SOURCES OF MUSIC

Production libraries include Megatrax, Killer Tracks and Warner Chappell, among many others. TV stations often use this music for advertising, commercials, bumps, intros, and background. Typically, the library has all rights to both the sound recording and the underlying musical composition. The libraries typically provide licenses for the synch rights to music, allowing the library music to be incorporated into videos. Using a library can result in savings on PRO fees paid by local TV if a station can take advantage of this license. See Section 8. If a station has a per program license, it is sometimes cheaper to buy both performance rights and synchronization rights from the library.

SECTION 5

THE PLAYERS

While understanding the terminology related to music licensing is vital, it's even more important to identify the music licensing players who participate in the exchange of billions of dollars every year.

Whether someone is a Spotify subscriber, listens to over-the-air radio in their car, or produces TV program segments with music, chances are they have never thought about the business infrastructure that underlies the music created and produced for the general public's pleasure.

There are a variety of different people and organizations that pull strings in various ways. Some represent artists: some are music users: and yet others aim to regulate the business and prevent abuses of market power. Let's look at each one in turn.

MUSIC CREATORS

Songwriters and Composers—While these terms are often used interchangeably, there's a difference. Typically, a songwriter creates both the lyrics (words) and the melody of a song. According to the Guinness Book of World Records, the most successful songwriters in terms of No. 1 singles are John Lennon and Paul McCartney.

Composers typically write the music but not the lyrics. Famous composers with whom you might be familiar include Beethoven, John Williams, George Gershwin, Scott Joplin, and Aaron Copeland.

Songwriters and composers may or may not perform and record their own music. Most contemporary recording artists perform and record works created by songwriters and composers whose names you probably don't know. Of course, a few folks are famous songwriters who are equally renowned recording artists such as Pharrell Williams, John Legend, Taylor Swift, and Dolly Parton.

Many songs have more than one composer or songwriter. These are known as joint works.

Recording Artists—Performers who record music—whether the music they write themselves or music written by others—are called recording artists. Their recorded work is called a sound recording.

Among the famous performers who never wrote any of the songs they recorded and performed are Elvis Presley, Frank Sinatra, and Diana Ross. Some artists perform or record "cover" versions of famous songs that were originally recorded by someone else. Of course, a license is typically required for this.

Record companies usually pay recording artists pursuant to an individually negotiated contract. However, SoundExchange pays the recording artists directly or their representatives for the use of their music by certain noninteractive streaming services, including satellite radio provider Sirius XM and online radio services like the free service offered by Pandora.

SoundExchange, Inc. (SoundExchange) collects royalties from these noninteractive services and, after taking a "cut," pays out the royalties to the recording artists and record labels that own or control the copyrighted sound recordings that were performed on these services. SoundExchange also litigates on behalf of the recorded music industry in Copyright Royalty Board (CRB) proceedings. More on this in Section 10.

Records, CDs, and digital downloads have become less popular in recent years. Recording artists now rely heavily on interactive music streaming services to distribute their music to the public.

REPRESENTATIVES OF MUSIC CREATORS

Before getting into the specifics of different types of representatives, here's an overview: music creators—such as songwriters, composers, and recording artists—frequently do not undertake the promotion, reproduction, and distribution of their recordings and compositions by themselves. A host of small and large publishers and record companies assist them with that.

Songwriters and composers typically transfer their musical works rights to record, perform, and distribute their musical works to music publishers, whose activities on behalf of the songwriters and composers are detailed below.

Public performance rights bestowed upon songwriters and composers by the copyright laws are not typically handled directly by the publishers. The publishers or the songwriters and composers are represented by the performance rights organizations (PROs) in the negotiation and license of public performance rights.

Composers can belong to only one PRO at a time. However, music publishers (which help exploit composers' works commercially) can be members of more than one, typically through different sub-entities.

Recording artists follow a different business and legal path. They generally transfer their sound recording rights to record labels. In turn, the labels oversee the production, promotion and licensing of the sound recording. The labels also handle the collection of revenues, including from sales of CDs, digital downloads and interactive streaming services usage. Then they pay the recording artists a percentage of the revenue after taking a "cut."

Music Publishers—Music publishers typically promote and license the musical works they own or control, collect royalties for the use of these musical works, and pay out to the songwriters their share of the royalties generated. Music publishers only handle the musical work, not the sound recording.

Songwriters and composers enter into negotiated agreements with music publishers to promote their works, and, in turn, the publishers get a share of the royalties. Many songs have multiple songwriters, and each can have their own publisher. The three major music publishers are Universal Music Publishing Group, Sony/ATV, and Warner/Chappell. See Section 3 for more.

The National Music Publishers Association (NMPA)—As stated on the organization's website, the NMPA is a trade association founded in 1917 that represents all American music publishers and their songwriting partners. "Its mission is to protect, promote, and advance the interests of music's creators...." For more information, see www.nmpa.org.

Record Labels/Record Companies –Typically, record labels handle the licensing for the sound recordings they own or control. There are exceptions for sound recording uses that qualify for the Section 112 and 114 statutory licenses. See Section 10 for more.

The largest record labels are Sony Music Group, Universal Music Group, and Warner Music Group.

PERFORMANCE RIGHTS ORGANIZATIONS

(also referred to as Performing Rights Societies)

Songwriters and composers receive by far the most compensation for their musical works from performance rights organizations or societies, commonly known as PROs. As previously noted, songwriters and composers often transfer the rights to their music to publishers. Music publishers who represent these music creators are members or affiliates of the PROs, as are their represented composers and songwriters.

Individual songwriters and composers who are not represented by a publishing company are also typically PRO members or affiliates.

PROs focus on performance rights. PROs do not handle sound recordings or compensate recording artists. PROs also do not get involved with synchronization or other reproduction rights licenses, which are discussed more fully in Section 12.

> PROs focus on performance rights. PROs do not handle sound recordings or compensate recording artists.

In effect, the PROs are "middlemen" between two different groups. One group includes songwriters, composers, and any publishers that represent them.

The second group includes entities that bring the music to the consumer. Bars and restaurants fall into that category, along with local radio stations, iHeartRadio, Apple Music, Spotify, local TV, Netflix, PBS, and concert promoters like LiveNation—to name just a few.

The PROs negotiate music performance rights license agreements on behalf of songwriters, composers, and publishers with those in the second group. Then the PROs distribute the fees generated as royalties to the composers, songwriters and publishers they represent after deducting a portion of the royalties received from licensees for administrative expenses. PROs only handle royalty payments from entities that "publicly perform" music. The performances can take place at live concerts. They also might show up on TV shows or digital streaming platforms. All are considered public performances.

The PROs typically take all the musical works in their repertories and bundle them into a single license known as a blanket license. The two most prominent PROs, ASCAP and BMI collectively have about 20 million musical works in their repertories as of this writing.

Joint writers can belong to different PROs. When that's the case, the PROs pay each writer their respective share of the royalties collected for individual musical works. The PROs might offer certain writers and publishers advances against future performance royalties to attract new members or affiliates.

Music users often take a blanket license from each PRO. Among their reasons for doing so is that the repertories of the different PROs do not overlap—each composer and songwriter only affiliates with one PRO. So it helps the user to avoid the risk of copyright infringement liability.

ASCAP and BMI collectively control approximately 90% of U.S. performing rights, according to some reports. However, the percentage of musical works performed by different media licensees (TV, radio, etc.) controlled by ASCAP and BMI varies significantly. Here's a summary of each PRO:

ASCAP—More formally known as the American Society of Composers, Authors and Publishers, ASCAP was the first PRO established in the United States. The nonprofit entity was formed in the early 1900s to manage the collection of fees for the public performance of music in bars, taverns, cabarets, and other entertainment venues, including piano playing in silent film theaters.

At the time, songwriters and publishers had no way of monitoring all of these somewhat private performances of their music and thus collecting royalties.

ASCAP hired a large group of licensing and collection agents to negotiate and collect fees from these establishments. As a result, songwriters and publishers were compensated for the public performance of their music.

According to the PRO's 2023 annual report, "ASCAP delivered a record-breaking $1.737 billion in revenue in the 2023 calendar year, an increase of $215 million, or 14.1% over the prior year, with $1.592 billion available to … songwriter, composer and music publisher members." ASCAP has more than 960,000 members according to a posting in 2023 on its website.

For more information, see www.ascap.com.

BMI—Officially known as Broadcast Music Inc., BMI was founded in 1939 by a group of broadcasters to provide an alternative to ASCAP, which had previously been the only game in town.

At the dawn of the music business, musicians' primary means of generating revenue was the sale of sheet music. Between 1902 and 1912, Guglielmo Marconi patented several inventions in wireless communication that led to the development of radio.

During the 1930s, radio was coming to prominence as a source of musical entertainment that threatened to weaken phonorecord sales and opportunities for "live" acts. ASCAP required radio stations to take blanket licenses granting the PRO a fixed percentage of each station's revenue, regardless of how much music the station played from ASCAP's repertory. In 1939, ASCAP announced a substantial increase in the revenue share that licensees would be required to pay.

Broadcasters took action by creating BMI. The new PRO's founders consisted of broadcast station executives. In early 2024, New Mountain Capital, a growth-oriented investment firm, acquired BMI and bought out the broadcast industry shareholders.

For the vast majority of music users today, BMI is not an alternative to ASCAP. Licenses from both organizations are typically needed.

Before the sale, BMI reported revenue of about $1.57 billion for the fiscal year ending June 30, 2022, and paid out about $1.47 billion to its songwriters, composer and publishers. Currently, BMI represents more than 1.4 million songwriters, composers, and publishers.

For more information, see www.bmi.com.

Global Music Rights (GMR)—When it was founded in 2013 by industry veteran Irving Azoff, GMR became the first new PRO to emerge in 75 years. According to its website, GMR is "an alternative to the performance rights model."

While the PRO represents far fewer writers and publishers than ASCAP or BMI, it has acquired some well-known composers' catalogs in the past few years. Music from Post Malone, Smokey Robinson, Prince, and Bon Jovi is all under its umbrella.

As will be described in later sections, GMR was in a costly and protracted antitrust legal battle with the Radio Music License Committee for several years.

GMR is a privately held, for-profit entity and, unlike ASCAP and BMI, is not subject to a Department of Justice (DOJ) consent decree discussed later in this Guide. For more information, see www.globalmusicrights.com.

SESAC—This one-time acronym is the PRO's official name today. Originally it was known as the Society of European Stage Authors and Composers. It is a for-profit, privately held performance rights organization in the United States.

SESAC's founder was a German immigrant who wanted to assist European stage authors and composers with their American public performance royalties. When it was established in 1930, SESAC became the second PRO in the United States.

SESAC has 30,000 songwriters and over 1 million compositions in its catalog and has become a more prominent PRO over the last two decades. Like GMR, SESAC is not subject to a DOJ consent decree. For more information, see www.sesac.com.

MUSIC USERS AND THEIR REPRESENTATIVES

The people and organizations that fall within this group are numerous. Let's look at the major ones, each in turn:

You and Me—We all listen to music.

Concert Promoters—Companies like LiveNation produce music concerts for recording artists. They need public performance licenses from the PROs to conduct their business.

Food and Entertainment Venues—Bars, restaurants, wineries, and hotels frequently play music in their establishments. When they do, these venues must obtain public performance licenses.

Digital Music Association (DiMA)—According to its website, DiMA represents "the world's leading audio streaming companies, whose innovations are driving the economic engine that saved and revitalized the music industry, bringing it forward from the depths of the harm caused by piracy into a brighter future."

The organization's member companies include Amazon, Apple Music, Google/YouTube, Pandora, and Spotify. Its mission is "to promote and protect the ability of music fans to legally engage with creative content whenever and wherever they want it, and for artists to more easily reach longtime fans and make new ones."

Digital music providers represented by DiMA require music licenses for rights described later in this Guide. For more information, see www.dima.org.

Radio Music License Committee (RMLC)—This organization represents the interests of the commercial radio industry on music licensing matters. It is structured as a 501(c)(6) nonprofit Tennessee corporation based in Nashville and has over 10,000 commercial radio station members. Its directors, who volunteer to serve without compensation, reflect a diverse group of station owners and management.

The RMLC represents its stations in their negotiation with the PROs for public performance licenses and aims to achieve fair and reasonable license fees. It is dedicated to negotiating licenses that reflect the realities of the current and changing state of the radio business.

When negotiations are concluded, the resulting license agreements are entered into by its members. When negotiations break down, RMLC also litigates on behalf of its members. For more information, see www.rmlc.org.

Television Music License Committee (TVMLC)—When it was founded in 1948, the TVMLC was a negotiating committee within the National Association of Broadcasters (NAB). It represented local television stations in their dealings with ASCAP. Over time, the committee separated from NAB, although NAB continues to advise TVMLC on government matters related to music licensing.

TVMLC is funded by voluntary contributions from the local television industry. It represents the collective interests of some 1,200 full power local commercial television stations—large and small—in the United States in negotiations with the PROs to secure fair and reasonable license fees and terms for the public performance of musical works on local television. It focuses exclusively on music performance rights licensing matters. When negotiations break down, the TVMLC has also assisted the local television industry in bringing federal "rate court" litigation, aiming to rein in the abuse of monopoly power of the PROs. TVMLC also assists stations to maximize local television stations' abilities to secure public performance rights in actual competitive market transactions.

For more information, see www.tvmlc.com.

MIC Coalition—This group, pronounced MIC like "mike" (as in microphone), is a group of associations whose members transmit licensed music in a variety of ways: over the nation's airwaves, through the internet, as well as in stores, hotels, restaurants, bars, and taverns throughout the U.S.

The Coalition is committed to a rational, sustainable, and transparent system that will drive the future of music and ensure that consumers have continued access to music across various platforms, venues, and services.

Its members include TVMLC, RMLC, NAB, DiMA, National Religious Broadcasters (NRB), and several dozen trade associations representing hotels, wineries, restaurants, and movie theaters, to name but a few.

The Coalition took an active role in response to Assistant Attorney General Makan Delrahim's suggestion in 2018 that the Department of Justice (DOJ) should review the ASCAP and BMI consent decrees again to determine if they were still useful, effective, or needed modification or even termination. See Section 14.

For more information, see www.mic-coalition.org.

National Association of Broadcasters (NAB)—As stated on www.nab.org, "The National Association of Broadcasters is the voice for the nation's radio and television broadcasters. As the premier trade association for broadcasters, NAB advances the interests of our members in federal government, industry, and public affairs; improves the quality and profitability of broadcasting; encourages content and technology innovation; and spotlights the important and unique ways stations serve their communities. NAB delivers value to our members through advocacy, education, and innovation."

NAB provides educational, legal, and government relations support to the RMLC and the TVMLC concerning public performance music licensing matters. Both organizations were originally a part of NAB, but now operate independently.

National Religious Broadcasters (NRB)—According to its website, NRB is an international association of Christian communicators with more than 1,100 member organizations reaching millions of viewers, listeners, and readers. As part of its service to members, NRB has its own music license committee, which is described below. The vast majority of its members are local radio stations.

With headquarters in Washington, D.C., near Capitol Hill, NRB maintains a close working relationship with the Federal Communications Commission (FCC), Congress, the courts, and the executive branch, representing the interests of NRB members and the people they serve.

Its website explains that NRB exists "to represent the Christian broadcasters' right to communicate the Gospel of Jesus Christ to a lost and dying world." For more information, visit www.nrb.org.

National Religious Broadcasters Music License Committee (NRBMLC)— NRBMLC represents full power AM and FM radio stations in the U.S. and its territories in music licensing negotiations. Its focus is to serve its authorized stations in negotiating fair and nondiscriminatory music licenses with the PROs and SoundExchange. The NRBMLC has, in recent years, been involved in proceedings to set rates and terms for music licenses for Internet streaming. This standing committee of the NRB has a noncommercial counterpart with a similar acronym: NRBNMLC.

ADMINISTRATORS

Mechanical Rights Administrators—Mechanical rights licenses and associated royalties cover the right to reproduce a composition by recording, manufacturing, and distributing the work. They are separate and distinct from performance licenses.

Royalties from mechanical rights licenses are paid to songwriters, composers, and music publishers when music is sold in physical form (such as CDs or vinyl) or as a digital download. Mechanical royalties are also owed when music is streamed on-demand via digital platforms like Spotify.

The mechanical right for musical works is subject to statutory licensing under section 115 of the Copyright Act. Many mechanical licenses are also issued and administered directly by music publishers in many cases. See Section 11 for more information.

Music Reports Inc. (MRI)—Originally a part of TVMLC, MRI assists local television broadcasters to take advantage of alternatives to the blanket licensing structures offered by ASCAP and BMI. The organization developed a music usage and information system that creates detailed reports on TV station music usage to submit to the PROs.

MRI operates the largest database of worldwide music rights and related business information. It represents major users of music, including HBO, Netflix, Pandora, Spotify, Amazon Music, iTunes, commercial TV networks, and hundreds of local TV stations.

The organization's clients receive expertise, assistance, and solutions related to music use licensing, administration, royalty accounting, along with software development and hosting.

For TV stations, MRI acts as a third-party administrator to assist stations that use a per program license to report music use to PROs. See Section 8 for more information about per program licenses.

SoundExchange—Congress authorized this nonprofit collective rights management organization to collect and distribute certain sound recording performance royalties.

Both featured and non-featured artists (and record companies representing them) receive royalties from SoundExchange for the noninteractive use of their sound recordings under the statutory licenses outlined in 17 U.S.C. Sections 112 and 114, which is discussed later in this Guide. See Section 10.

SoundExchange's board of directors is composed of artists, artist representatives, and sound recording copyright owners. On its website, SoundExchange states that it is an advocate for music licensing reform. As of 2023, it had paid more than $10 billion to recording artists and rights owners.

For more information, see www.soundexchange.com.

UNITED STATES GOVERNMENT

U.S. Department of Justice (DOJ)—The mission of the Antitrust Division of the DOJ is to "promote economic competition through enforcing and providing guidance on antitrust laws and principles," according to its website.

The DOJ is responsible for negotiating and enforcing the consent decrees that govern ASCAP and BMI in their licensing of music public performance rights. From time to time, the Department has reviewed the operation and effectiveness of the consent decrees. More information on that review can be found in Section 14.

U.S. Copyright Office and Congress—Periodically, congressional committees and the U.S. Copyright Office review current laws. They've introduced and passed new laws that impact music usage. Among them is the recently enacted Music Modernization Act described in detail in Section 11.

Copyright Royalty Board—This three-judge panel sits within the U.S. Library of Congress. It determines rates and terms for statutory copyright licenses and presides over proceedings related to the distribution of certain royalties.

These statutory licenses cover the use of sound recordings by noninteractive digital streaming services, satellite radio, and others. And they also cover certain "mechanical" (reproduction) musical works licenses. However, the Board does not preside over disputes between the PROs and licensees.

U.S. Federal Court in the Southern District of New York— Disputes under the ASCAP and BMI consent decrees are generally brought and heard in this court. These consent decrees, covered in Section 14, directly impact the music performance licenses of local radio and TV broadcasters. The court has a long history of reviewing and making laws pertaining to music licensing.

LAW FIRMS AND ECONOMISTS

As you will realize when you reach the end of this Guide, music licensing has a long and extensive history involving complex licensing negotiations and, when all else fails, litigation.

Negotiations and litigation—particularly antitrust and rate-setting litigation—require the engagement of lawyers who have knowledge in three distinct areas: antitrust, copyright, and music rights.

The statutory provisions of the U.S. Copyright laws related to music licensing are complicated and detailed. It's safe to say that there are probably not more than a dozen lawyers in the country who can claim meaningful expertise in the field of music use licensing.

Litigation involving rate setting and the consent decrees often requires the use of expert witnesses, who are primarily economists. The learning curve is steep, so it's not unusual to see the same law firms and economists involved in major negotiations, administrative hearings, and litigation.

SECTION 6

MUSICAL WORKS: PUBLIC PERFORMANCE RIGHTS–GENERAL

National TV networks, public venues, religious broadcasters, and streaming services must all secure public performance rights to do business.

The next few sections of this Guide will discuss the most significant copyright right for all music media platforms—public performance rights. More dollars flow from music consumers to music creators and their representatives because of public performance rights than from any other copyright law protection.

The public performance of musical works can occur in:

- TV and radio shows;
- Digital streaming platforms;
- Film exhibition;
- Bars, restaurants, retail stores, and other venues.

The performance rights organizations (PROs) issue licenses for the public performance of musical works on behalf of music publishers and songwriters. But they do not license the rights in sound recordings, discussed later in this Guide.

> More dollars flow from music consumers to music creators and their representatives because of public performance rights than from any other copyright law protection.

NATIONAL CABLE AND TV NETWORKS AND PUBLIC BROADCASTING TV

TV that is not considered local—such as cable and TV broadcast networks—usually obtains public performance rights to the musical works in programs under blanket licenses from the PROs. The license agreement terms and fees are negotiated in private commercial transactions and are typically confidential.

PROs negotiate public performance rights license agreements and collect license fees from both premium cable channels (like HBO, Cinemax, and Showtime) and basic-cable channels (like MTV, USA Network, CNN, and Lifetime).

Large broadcast networks—such as ABC, CBS, and NBC— also obtain performance licenses from the PROs for the music in the programs they produce themselves—everything from "The Voice" to National Football League telecasts to soap operas. These rights are passed along to the individual stations that broadcast the network programming, typically in affiliation agreements.

ASCAP and BMI currently have network licenses with ABC, CBS, and NBC/Univision under negotiated network license agreements. The Fox and CW networks do not currently have a network license with the PROs. Instead, local TV stations that carry Fox and CW shows have licenses with the PROs covering music performances in all their programming, including the programming provided by these networks. These are licenses negotiated by TVMLC.

The PROs have privately negotiated blanket licenses for public performance rights with the Corporation for Public Broadcasting (CPB) that cover local, affiliated public broadcasting stations. These licenses pertain to any programming produced by CPB or its affiliates.

BUSINESS ESTABLISHMENTS

Business establishments like bars, restaurants, hotels, stores, and similar venues have two options. They can get public performance rights to play musical works from the PROs. Or they can obtain the necessary rights from certain services that provide the business establishment with music, including the required performance rights.

These establishments face a significant challenge when obtaining the licenses directly from the PROs: the business owners are legally limited to playing music represented by the PROs that have issued them a license.

While each PRO has a searchable database of the musical works they cover, it is not always updated, comprehensive, or user-friendly. As a result, venue owners are vulnerable to copyright infringement claims. The safest bet for most venues is to pay licensing fees to all PROs, which is an expensive endeavor. Of course, what happens when new PROs are created?

The PROs determine the venues' annual licensing fees by a variety of factors. Here are some of them:

- Single-unit versus multi-unit operation;
- Square footage of the establishment;
- Customer capacity of the venue;
- Number of nights music is played;
- Whether music played is recorded or live;
- Whether a cover charge is collected.

As mentioned, business owners can opt to not take licenses from the PROs. Instead, they can work with a service that provides the venue with music and has paid the appropriate license fees on their behalf.

It is not sufficient to use an individual (as opposed to a business establishment) subscription to a music service like Pandora or Spotify and then play that service over speakers in the establishment.

Multiple music providers offer a service that includes paying licensing fees to PROs on behalf of the business owner. The owner pays the music service a monthly or yearly fee and can feel secure that all the songs played in their establishment are appropriately licensed.

Always check with a music provider, but for the most part, the licenses they obtain do not include coverage for any live music or music that isn't played through the device they provide.

RADIO

Both over-the-air radio stations and satellite radio must secure licenses to publicly perform musical works. Radio obtains its licenses through the PROs. For detailed history and information about broadcast radio's negotiations with the PROs for public performance licenses, see Section 7.

DIGITAL STREAMING

There are both interactive and noninteractive services that fall under the digital streaming "umbrella."

Interactive streaming services include Spotify, Apple, Google, and Amazon. They allow the listener to pick exactly which song they want to hear. Such services have two options to obtain public performance licenses: either from the PROs or directly from music publishers.

The PROs' revenue from these sources is growing rapidly and has surpassed what they receive from local broadcast radio and TV.

Noninteractive streaming services include Pandora's flagship, ad-supported, "lean back" service and simulcast streams of over-the-air radio broadcasts. They have the same public performance license options as the interactive streamers: either obtain licenses through the PROs or directly through music publishers. Typically, these licenses include a fixed fee generally expressed as a percentage of service revenue or a flat dollar amount.

RELIGIOUS BROADCASTERS

Like other television broadcasters, religious television station broadcasters must secure public performance rights for musical works and any necessary synchronization rights. Many commercial, religious television broadcasters are represented by the TVMLC in its negotiations for public performance licenses with the PROs.

Religious radio broadcasters also obtain public performance rights licenses from the PROs. If any religious radio broadcaster is making their radio feed available through online streaming (sometimes referred to as simulcast streaming), they must also secure the necessary sound recording rights.

The fees and terms for the necessary sound recording rights are typically set by the Copyright Royalty Board (CRB) every five years. The NRBMLC represents religious radio broadcasters and participates in the CRB rate-setting proceedings.

Sound Recording rights are covered in Section 10 of this Guide.

QUESTIONS FROM OUR AUDIENCE

Q: If I operate a hotel and have a TV in the lobby, do the TV station licenses cover this public performance or do I need additional licenses? If I own a bar, and have a subscription to Pandora or Spotify, am I covered when I play those services over the speaker system?

A: No, and probably no (unless your business subscribes to a specific business establishment music service). Hotels, bars, and retail establishments that have a television on in the establishment cannot rely on public performance licenses granted to TV stations to cover the public performances of music in the programming broadcast over the television. Similarly, those establishments cannot use an individual subscription to Pandora or Spotify and play that music over its speaker system.

However, many music services do offer "business establishment services." These services are different from the subscriptions that services such as Pandora or Spotify make available to individuals (which do not grant any public performance rights to the subscriber), and often do cover the public performance rights licenses necessary to play the music they provide in the establishment that holds the subscription. If you opt to use a business establishment service subscription, you should check the terms carefully to make sure they grant you all of the necessary rights.

SECTION 7

MUSICAL WORKS: PUBLIC PERFORMANCE RIGHTS— BROADCAST RADIO

The radio industry has its own history of legal battles with the PROs, which are separate and distinct from those of other media.

Local radio and TV stations have a long history of negotiating with performance rights organizations (PROs). Both the Radio Music License Committee and the Television Music License Committee (RMLC and TVMLC) were originally part of the National Association of Broadcasters (NAB). They now operate as independent entities from the NAB and each other.

RMLC represents the interests of the commercial radio industry on music licensing matters. It is structured as a 501(c)(6) nonprofit Tennessee corporation based outside Nashville. Its directors, who volunteer to serve without compensation, reflect a diverse group of station owners and management. William (Bill) Velez, a veteran of the music industry, is the organization's long-time executive director.

This voluntary-membership organization has negotiated licenses with certain PROs that are pertinent to some 10,000 commercial, over-the-air, terrestrial radio stations.

To broadcast music, local radio stations must get public performance licenses from PROs. These are primarily blanket licenses, although program period licenses are increasingly used for news/talk-formatted stations. (The equivalent in the TV business is called a "per program" license.) Unlike local TV, local, commercial, over-the-air, terrestrial radio stations pay most PROs for performance licenses based on a percentage of advertising revenue. As a result, payments to these PROs go up and down over time. Typically, license agreements are five years.

Music public performance licensing by local radio, like local TV, is regulated to some degree by the ASCAP and BMI consent decrees further discussed in Section 14. When voluntary negotiations between RMLC and ASCAP or BMI break down, the matter can be brought to the Federal District Court of New York (Southern District), which acts as a "rate court."

The objective of the RMLC is to achieve fair and reasonable license fees with music licensing organizations (such as ASCAP, BMI, and SESAC) on behalf of radio stations. As noted on its website, the RMLC attempts to negotiate licenses that reflect the realities of the radio business's current and changing state. Some of the RMLC's negotiation goals with the PROs include:

- Implementation of licenses that accurately reflect industry economic performance, with the least amount of administrative intrusion;

- Program period and/or blanket license "carve-out" alternatives that offer the potential for further fee discounting based upon a station's ability to make strategic music programming choices and/or license music directly from copyright owners;

- Negotiation of licenses that provide the broadest scope of rights possible with respect to new media—such as streaming, high-definition (HD) multicasting, mobile, and other "through-to-the-listener" applications;
- Continuation of the mandated RMLC funding mechanism.

Radio stations that benefit from the RMLC's work pay a fee to RMLC that funds the organization's operations and pays for the cost of the litigation and/or negotiations that led to the license agreements.

Like local TV, the radio industry has at times found itself in litigation with the PROs. Below we describe only the most recent settlements and developments between RMLC and the PROs to give a general idea of how fees are determined.

ASCAP

In a press release issued in December 2016, RMLC and ASCAP announced the following: "a new five-year agreement through 2021 that sets the rates payable by over 10,000 of America's commercial terrestrial radio stations to publicly perform more than 10.5 million musical works in the ASCAP repertory. The RMLC represents the vast majority of the nation's radio stations, and ASCAP represents 600,000 songwriters, composers and music publisher members whose songs and compositions comprise the largest catalog of music played on commercial AM/FM radio of any performing rights organization in the United States."

Unlike previous voluntary license agreements, this license's terms are confidential except to ASCAP, RMLC and its stations.

This license expired on December 31, 2021. The RMLC and ASCAP agreed to an interim license, which became effective on January 1, 2022, and generally extended the terms of the prior license until a new agreement is reached. License fees paid during this interim period may be adjusted retroactively once the parties have reached a new agreement.

On June 15, 2022, the RMLC filed a rate court petition against both ASCAP and BMI in the Southern District of New York, seeking a determination of reasonable fees and terms for a license covering the period

January 1, 2022 through December 31, 2026. The RMLC asserted that under the Music Modernization Act (MMA), enacted in 2018, a rate court action could now be brought against ASCAP and BMI jointly. ASCAP and BMI disagreed. Ultimately, on August 3, 2023, ASCAP was dismissed from the action, and the RMLC brought a new separate rate proceeding against ASCAP only; as of September 2024, the litigation is ongoing.

BMI

After the license agreement between RMLC and BMI expired December 31, 2016, there were protracted voluntary negotiations. In May 2019, RMLC filed a petition in the Federal District Court in the Southern District of New York, to set reasonable final rates and terms retroactive to January 1, 2017. In April 2020, the two sides reached a settlement agreement and submitted it to the court for approval before going to trial.

The new license agreement covered the period January 1, 2017 through December 31, 2021. It preserves the scope of rights contained in the previous license for over-the-air broadcasts, simulcast streaming and website activity as well as HD multicasting. Here are some of the agreement's highlights:

- Going forward, for terrestrial broadcast/simulcast transmissions, BMI receives a fee equivalent to 1.78% of a station's ad revenue, less a standard deduction of 12%. Digital revenues are subject to an increased deduction of up to 30%, an increase from 25% under the prior license.
- The per program (or program period) license applicable to many talk-formatted stations was retained. It involves a base fee of 0.31% of revenues, less the same standard deductions detailed above.
- New media rights coverage continues. The license covers, among other things, performances on websites and those heard through smartphones, and other wireless devices.
- The radio industry was obligated to pay a one-time $5 million fee to BMI by December 31, 2020 to cover litigation costs. The industry-wide allocation of this fee was tied to station amounts due to BMI for the calendar year 2019, on a straight pro-rata basis.

In its press release, RMLC stated that 1) during the course of negotiations, BMI was able to substantiate that its affiliates' radio spin share had increased relative to ASCAP's; 2) the 1.78% headline rate is in line with what the industry has paid to ASCAP and BMI for decades; and 3) the percentage-of-revenue license structure means that fees will adjust along with station revenues during these uncertain economic times.

This license expired on December 31, 2021. As with ASCAP, the RMLC and BMI entered into an interim license agreement effective January 1, 2022, which likewise extended the prior terms until the successful negotiation of a new license.

As mentioned above, the RMLC filed a joint rate court proceeding against ASCAP and BMI in 2022. BMI asserted that the joint action violated its consent decree. The Court stayed the proceeding pending a ruling on whether a joint rate proceeding against both ASCAP and BMI was permitted by BMI's consent decree and the MMA. The judge with jurisdiction over BMI's consent decree analyzed the language in the MMA and the decree and concluded that it is not permissible to bring a petition against BMI and ASCAP jointly. Following this determination, the Court resumed the rate-court proceeding, and ASCAP was removed as a party (but, as noted above, a separate rate proceeding was brought against ASACP). As of September 2024, the litigation is ongoing.

SESAC

As previously noted, SESAC is not subject to a DOJ consent decree as are ASCAP and BMI.

In October 2012, RMLC filed an antitrust lawsuit against SESAC. It was settled in July 2015 and called for constraints on SESAC that are similar to some of those imposed on ASCAP and BMI by their consent decrees. While there is no "rate court" for SESAC, it did agree to go to binding arbitration if the RMLC and SESAC cannot reach agreement on license fees.

With the antitrust suit settlement, fees paid by radio stations changed from a fixed, rate-card structure to a variable structure. Music-formatted stations were required to pay a rate of 0.2557% of revenue. All-talk stations received a discount of 77.5% off that rate. The license covers over-the-air, HD multicasting, and simulcast streaming (mirroring the ASCAP/BMI licenses).

RMLC and SESAC announced a subsequent license agreement on August 24, 2020. In their joint press release, the two organizations explained that it "sets the rates payable by the majority of America's commercial terrestrial radio stations to publicly perform works in the SESAC repertory, effective Jan. 1, 2019 through Dec. 31, 2022." The agreement rolled-forward the rates and terms from the prior license, including:

- A blanket license fee of 0.2557% of net revenue;
- An All-Talk rate of 0.0575% of revenue.

As before, this agreement applies to stations' over-the-air broadcasts, simulcast streams, and HD signals.

This license expired at the end of 2022. The RMLC and SESAC entered into an interim license carrying forward the prior license fees and terms. Following months of negotiations, on April 3, 2023, SESAC commenced an arbitration proceeding to determine license fees for the 2023 – 2026 period. The arbitration hearing occurred in mid-2024. On November 1, 2024, it was announced that the arbitrators had issued their decision, and had set a rate payable by music format stations of 0.2824% of revenue.

GMR

As earlier described, GMR is a relatively new PRO, formed in 2013. At its inception, GMR sought out the RMLC to discuss licensing terms that GMR could offer to radio stations. During those discussions, GMR emphasized that January 1, 2017 was the deadline for stations to obtain a license. On that date, stations would no longer have a license to broadcast most of the works in the GMR catalog as, by then, those works would no longer be licensed by ASCAP and BMI and could only be licensed by GMR.

As previously noted, composers and songwriters can—and do—change PRO affiliations/memberships and that is what happened here. Composers and songwriters previously affiliated with ASCAP and BMI agreed to join GMR and their catalogs of compositions moved with them and became licensable by GMR to radio stations effective January 1, 2017.

Radio stations believed that the license fees GMR were demanding were much too high and not remotely "reasonable." As a result, the RMLC filed a lawsuit against GMR in November 2016 in the United States District Court for the Eastern District of Pennsylvania alleging that GMR was violating the antitrust laws, including because it was facilitating an illegal price fixing conspiracy and because it was abusing its market power.

Shortly thereafter, GMR filed its own lawsuit against the RMLC in the United States District Court for the Central District of California alleging that the RMLC was violating the antitrust laws by acting as an illegal cartel for the purpose of artificially depressing license fees for publicly performing music on the radio.

While the dueling lawsuits were pending, GMR offered radio stations an interim fee license effective January 1, 2017, although the rates and terms of this interim license were not the product of negotiation with the RMLC. GMR subsequently offered several extensions of this interim license.

The Pennsylvania Court overseeing the lawsuit brought by the RMLC ruled that it lacked jurisdiction to hear the RMLC's complaint on March 29, 2019 and, as a result, it transferred the RMLC's case to federal court in California, where it was consolidated with GMR's lawsuit against the RMLC.

After several more years of litigation, in early 2022, the RMLC and GMR announced that they reached a settlement agreement, which included a license commencing April 1, 2022 that would be made available to all RMLC-represented radio stations. The fees and terms of this license are confidential.

QUESTIONS FROM OUR AUDIENCE

Q: My local radio or TV station wants to host a local children's choir to sing Christmas carols on air during the holidays. Is this ok?

A: Probably, especially in the context of radio broadcasts. Many Christmas carols are in the public domain, and public domain music can be used without a license. And, even if not in the public domain, so long as you have licenses from all of the PROs, you likely have the necessary public performance rights. But for television stations, in addition to PRO licenses covering the performance rights, you also need to obtain synchronization rights for any music that is not in the public domain if you intend to create an audiovisual recording of the broadcast for later viewing.

Q: My local radio or TV station wants to broadcast a worship service? Am I covered?

A: Probably, in the context of radio broadcasts. Some (and possibly all) of the music used in a worship service may be in the public domain. For this music, no licenses are needed. And, even if not in the public domain, so long as you have licenses from all of the PROs, you likely have the necessary public performance rights. For television stations, in addition to PRO licenses covering the performance rights, you would also need synchronization rights for any music that is not in the public domain if you intend to create an audiovisual recording of the broadcast for later viewing.

SECTION 8

MUSICAL WORKS: PUBLIC PERFORMANCE RIGHTS—BROADCAST TV

TELEVISION
MUSIC
LICENSE
COMMITTEE, LLC
RESOURCE, REPRESENTATION, ADVOCACY

The licensing that local TV needs to broadcast its programming is complex, critical, and costly. We explain below and show how TVMLC works on behalf of stations.

INTRODUCTION

Every program aired on local TV should have performance rights cleared for the copyrighted music that's used. In addition, producers generally need to clear synchronization rights—which involves "synching up" music to audiovisual content. That right, along with master use licenses—required if a producer wants to use an actual pre-recorded sound recording of a musical work—is covered in other sections of this Guide.

If you work for one of 1,200 local TV stations across the country, the license fees that your company pays ASCAP, BMI, and SESAC for performance rights probably are not negotiated by your purchasing or legal department. The Television Music License Committee (TVMLC or the Committee) handles those duties. This Section will give you a brief overview of the organization and explain why you pay, and what you pay, performance rights organizations (PROs).

TVMLC'S HISTORY AND MISSION

When the first ASCAP television licenses were negotiated in the 1940s, it was a reasonably cordial procedure. The PRO initially offered free rights to television broadcasters. That changed in 1948 when ASCAP terminated the free licenses.

Negotiations between local TV with ASCAP became contentious. The PRO continually demanded fee increases. Stations acquiesced to avoid copyright infringement claims. The creation of BMI as an alternative PRO did not ease the tension.

In response to the growing challenge, the National Association of Broadcasters (NAB) appointed a subcommittee, known as the All-Industry Television Station Music License Committee, or the Television Committee. It negotiated with ASCAP over the terms of a new form of license—a per program license—for local television stations. The Committee was unable to reach an agreement with ASCAP. In 1951, the Committee commenced a rate court proceeding under the provisions of the recently amended ASCAP consent decree (known as the Voice of Alabama proceeding). This was the beginning of a long, and sometimes contentious and litigious, relationship between local television stations and the PROs.

The next major event in the history of local TV's relationship with the PROs was the Buffalo Broadcasting proceeding described in Section 13. In this case, the court held, among other things, that ASCAP needed to provide local TV stations with economically viable alternatives to the blanket license previously offered. After this ruling, stations that took the per program license alternative could license at least some of the music they use directly from their rightsholders. The court set the terms and structure for such a license.

Eventually, the Television Committee was spun off from NAB and became TVMLC. It is a nonprofit trade association representing full-power, commercial television stations in the United States and its territories in negotiations for music performing rights licenses with ASCAP, BMI, and SESAC.

Through a settlement of a lawsuit filed by some broadcasters and funded by TVMLC, SESAC has agreed to negotiate industry-wide licenses with the Committee through 2035.

TVMLC's negotiations result in music performing rights licenses that stations sign with the PROs. The Committee designs and administers the formula for allocating industry-wide fees among all stations that take the licenses negotiated by the Committee (the vast majority of local television stations). This is subject to the agreement of a given PRO or court approval.

After stations sign their license agreements, TVMLC tries to resolve problems between stations and the PROs when they arise. The Committee also serves as a resource to local TV broadcasters, answering questions and providing other music licensing assistance. When negotiation with a PRO is unsuccessful, TVMLC funds and helps manage legal proceedings on behalf of the local television industry, such as copyright rate court proceedings and private antitrust litigation.

TVMLC is not a member organization and is funded through voluntary contributions. The Committee is made up of volunteer representatives from television stations and broadcasting groups throughout the country. They work at both large and small market stations as well as affiliates and independents. TVMLC also represents local, religious broadcast stations if they are full power and commercial.

The industry-wide licenses negotiated by TVMLC cover the music used

> TVMLC tries to resolve problems between stations and the PROs when they arise. The Committee also serves as a resource to local TV broadcasters, answering questions and providing other music licensing assistance. When negotiation with a PRO is unsuccessful, TVMLC funds and helps manage legal proceedings on behalf of the local television industry.

> The industry-wide licenses negotiated by TVMLC cover the music used in station programming and advertisements broadcast on primary channels and digital multicast channels, streamed on station websites, and provided to third party digital platforms.

in station programming and advertisements broadcast on primary channels and digital multicast channels, streamed on station websites, and provided to third party digital platforms.

The Committee represents local TV stations whether they make a contribution or not. However, the TVMLC has negotiated an allocation adjustment with ASCAP that incentivizes all stations that use the ASCAP industry-wide license negotiated by the Committee to participate in funding the Committee's efforts.

Under that ASCAP adjustment, stations that do not contribute or contribute less than the industry average of contributions are charged an additional fee. That added revenue is then credited back to stations that contribute more than the industry average.

OBTAINING PERFORMANCE RIGHTS

The ABC, CBS, NBC, and Univision networks negotiate (with the PROs) and pay for music performance rights for the music in the programming they distribute to their local station affiliates that are "through-to-the-viewer." Their local affiliates' transmission of those national shows is covered under the PRO licenses with the networks and the local stations do not need to separately secure licenses for the music in this programming.

As a result, ABC, CBS, NBC, and Univision affiliates need music performance rights only for their locally produced, non-network programming, along with rights related to advertising and syndicated programming.

The Fox, CW and MY networks do not negotiate "through-to-the-viewer" license for their network shows with the PROs. TV stations affiliated with these networks must separately obtain music performance rights for all their programming (including network programming) from PROs.

Generally, agreements for syndicated programming do NOT include the performance rights for the music contained in the shows. TV stations sometimes obtain music performance rights directly from the syndicators or from companies like Music Reports Inc. (MRI), which negotiate with the syndicators and get performance rights for music in such popular syndicated shows as "Wheel of Fortune" and "Jeopardy."

To sum it up, all local TV stations must independently obtain music performance rights from the PROs for all local programming, syndicated programming, promos, public service announcements (PSAs), and advertising. Depending on what network they're affiliated with, stations may need to clear performance rights for the network programming they transmit. That's where TVMLC comes in.

FEES AND LICENSE TERMS

When TVMLC negotiates public performance music licenses with the PROs, the terms include one industry-wide fee. The cost is split between the 1200+ stations that TVMLC represents. The license typically lasts three to five years. Without these licenses, local TV stations cannot practically operate or broadcast.

TV stations pay license fees to each PRO on either a blanket or per program basis.

A blanket license allows a station to broadcast any of the songs included in the repertory of a given PRO for a single fee. This provides a broadcaster with flexibility in deciding what music to use and protects a station against claims of copyright infringement by publishers or composers for performances of music in the PRO's repertory.

> In recent years, courts have required ASCAP and BMI to offer music users alternatives to the blanket license with fees that reflect the user's direct and source licensing activity.

Historically, blanket license fees were pre-determined. There was no fee credit or "carve-out" to reflect any licenses stations obtained directly from publishers or composers or through program suppliers.

In recent years, courts have required ASCAP and BMI to offer music users alternatives to the blanket license with fees that reflect the user's direct and source licensing activity. Currently, ASCAP offers television broadcasters an alternative blanket license (ABL) from which many stations benefit; and all three PROs (ASCAP, BMI and SESAC) offer a per program license option. BMI offers an adjustable-fee blanket license (AFBL). For more information on these options for local TV stations, contact TVMLC.

A per program license gives a station the same copyright infringement protection they get from the blanket license. However, the way the fees are calculated and the obligations to keep records of music use are different. Under this license form, a station is still entitled to broadcast any music it wants from the ASCAP, BMI, or SESAC repertories. But the station pays a fee that varies. It depends on the number of programs that include any music from a given PRO's repertory that is not otherwise licensed.

If a station seeks a license for music on a per program basis, it pays two types of fees. One is a set fee for commercials and other "incidental and ambient" uses of music. Secondly, the station pays for music used in programs that have not been separately licensed from individual copyright holders or from program producers—for example, the producer of a network or syndicated show.

Under a per program license, a station files detailed monthly reports with the PRO showing what programs it aired that month and which ones contained music from the PRO. By clearing rights directly with composers, publishers, or suppliers, a station can pay lower total fees to the PRO than they would pay under a standard blanket license.

If a program includes at least one second or "needle drop" of uncleared music (other than incidental or ambient music) from a song in the PRO's repertory, it would be subject to the full fee payable for that program.

The costs climb if a program includes both ASCAP and BMI music. In that instance, a station would pay a full per program fee to both PROs. On the other hand, if BMI represented all the music in a given program, the station would have no fee obligation to ASCAP.

The per program license is an essential licensing option to stations because it allows stations to engage in actual competitive transactions for music performance rights, which, in many cases, can bring license fees down. ASCAP, BMI and SESAC do not have exclusive rights with their members or affiliates. So, composers and music publishers can make separate deals for the use of their music in particular shows. This injection of competition in the licensing of music performance rights has been a central mission of TVMLC since its founding.

There are tradeoffs. Under the per program license, the starting fee is higher than the blanket fee the station would otherwise pay. But there is the opportunity to reduce that fee with each program the station "clears." Also, stations have greater recordkeeping and reporting requirements since they are responsible for tracking and providing music use information concerning every program they broadcast.

Third-party administrators such as Music Reports Inc. can analyze a TV station's music use and determine whether the station can save money by switching from a blanket to a per program license. There are alternate blanket license options for stations that do not qualify for the per program license option. Contact TVMLC for more information.

It is possible to obtain public performance rights directly from the music publishers. Some local TV stations do this for specific programs. If libraries provide performance rights (for an extra fee over and above synch rights), this is another way that stations can save money through the per program license.

CALCULATING THE FEES

TVMLC, on behalf of the stations it represents, negotiates an industry-wide blanket license fee with each PRO. That fee must be split in a reasonable and fair way among all the local TV stations.

TVMLC designs the method for allocating industry-wide blanket license fees for ASCAP, BMI or SESAC among the stations, and then performs an annual calculation of the individual station fees. The industry-wide blanket license fee is divided among all stations based on market size and ratings.

This methodology involves a two-step process. First, the industry-wide fee is split among individual markets, proportionate to market size. Then the fee for a given market is divided among stations there, based on a three-year ratings average. Each year the oldest set of ratings books is dropped, and the newest set is added. If either its market size or its share of audience within a market increases, a station's fees could increase.

For stations using the per program license, the blanket license fee allocated to those stations is used as a starting point. Calculations are made to that blanket license fee to account for cleared music and thus savings from the blanket license fee are obtained.

ASCAP, BMI AND SESAC

Stations don't produce the majority of shows they air. And stations are responsible for obtaining licenses for the public performance of copyrighted musical works in the programs they air, including for some network (for Fox, CW, MY, etc.) and all syndicated shows.

Stations cannot change the music embedded in content provided by others. They are contractually prohibited from doing so. The producers and syndicators of such programming do not obtain public performance rights licenses. That is the stations' responsibility.

In a sense, the stations' hands are tied. Because they must secure public performance rights licenses *after* the music has already been irrevocably embedded in the programming, stations have no meaningful ability to negotiate with composers and publishers over fees and terms. And they have no ability to change the music if a rightsholder demands an exorbitant license fee. This is often referred to as the "music in the can" problem.

There is no way of knowing all the music that is used in TV programming aired locally; who wrote that music; and the composer or publisher's PRO affiliation. Therefore, the only safe way to prevent copyright infringement lawsuits is to get a license from all PROs.

SETTLING FEE DISAGREEMENTS

When negotiations breakdown between the TVMLC and ASCAP or BMI, either party can bring a rate court action. A federal court judge hears arguments from both sides and establishes "reasonable" license fees based on the evidence.

These cases can sometimes take years. While waiting for a decision, the parties agree on interim license fees.

WHO'S IN CHARGE?

You might ask, "Who are the people involved in the negotiations? How do I know that they really care about my station and our limited budgets?"

Local TV station representatives sign written authorizations that give TVMLC permission to negotiate with the PROs on their behalf. TVMLC represents stations regardless of whether they contribute to TVMLC or not. When licenses are finalized, each station can take the license, but it is under no obligation to do so.

Representatives of stations on the Committee make decisions about license fees, license terms, allocation of fees, and litigation alternatives. Some members represent small market stations and small broadcast groups, and other members represent large broadcast companies like Hearst Television, Nexstar Media Group, and NBCUniversal.

PARTING THOUGHTS

The revenue generated by the local broadcast industry for the PROs has shrunk considerably over time as a percentage of the PROs' total revenue stream. This is due in part to the stations' audience erosion, as consumers flock to alternative sources of programming, such as Netflix and Hulu, which pay license fees to the PROs. Licenses between the PROs and these "new media" groups are confidential, and the negotiations have not triggered extensive litigation.

While there are many pages devoted to public performance licenses for local TV in this Guide, I encourage you to visit our website, www.tvmlc.com, for more information.

QUESTIONS FROM OUR AUDIENCE

Q: My TV station has a per program license. We have the synch rights to use popular music in our news bumps. Why shouldn't we start using them?

A: From a legal point of view, you can use the music in your news bumps as long as you have the synch rights (and master use rights, if needed, as described in Section 12). Financially, however, there may be a downside to doing so: if your station is taking per program licenses from one or more PROs, the savings your station otherwise gets under the per program licenses could be reduced, potentially significantly, by incorporating popular music into news bumps. For example, if the popular music you use in a bump is in the ASCAP repertory and you have not licensed that music through a means other than ASCAP, you will not receive any savings for that news program under an ASCAP per program license, even if all of the other music in the news program is licensed directly by the station. Check with your per program administrator such as MRI for more information.

Q: What is the status of license negotiations between TVMLC and the PROs?

A: As of November 2024, the status with each PRO is as follows. For SESAC, there are final licenses in place that cover the 2024-2027 period. For ASCAP, the most recent licenses expired on June 30, 2024. The Committee and ASCAP have reached an agreement in principle on new licenses that are expected to go through the end of 2027. The Committee expects that those licenses will be finalized before the end of 2024. Like ASCAP, the most recent BMI licenses expired on June 30, 2024. The Committee and BMI have entered into an "interim" agreement to ensure that local stations have the BMI license coverage they need while negotiations over new final license fees and terms continue.

Q: How about GMR? Does the Committee negotiate industry-wide licenses with GMR like it does with the other PROs?

A: Unlike ASCAP, BMI and SESAC, there is no TVMLC-negotiated, industry-wide license with GMR. That said, many of the TV stations and station groups that TVMLC represents have negotiated licenses with GMR. In mid-2024, GMR approached the Committee and requested assistance in developing a license structure for those local, commercial full-power stations that did not have a GMR license covering their local TV operations. The TVMLC agreed to act as an intermediary between those local stations and GMR to help ensure that local stations had the license coverage they need. As a result of those efforts, additional stations have taken GMR licenses.

SECTION 9

PRO MARKET SHARE

TVMLC counterbalances the PROs' private database records with an analysis that estimates market share among the various PROs.

It seems quite logical that the local TV industry should pay license fees based on a given PRO's share of the musical works used by stations. So, for example, if local TV pays the PROs a total of $100 annually, and the musical works of composers and publishers affiliated with SESAC make up 40% of the musical works broadcast on local TV, local TV should pay SESAC $40 annually.

While this seems reasonable, it is not so simple in practice. Each PRO analyzes and calculates its share of music in local TV differently, using different formulas and methodologies. Not surprisingly, these share estimates can be inflated, and their collective total can go well over 100%.

There is no public, universal database for all musical works that includes information from all PROs.

To get around this glaring void, the TVMLC commissions music use studies with assistance from economists, local stations, and Music Reports Inc. (MRI). In this way, TVMLC comes up with unbiased estimates of overall music use on local TV and the market shares of each PRO. The surveys are incredibly expensive and time-consuming but critically important.

For example, one annual TVMLC analysis might show that local TV stations used less music than they did the year before. If everything else was equal, that would call for a reduction in license fees. Or the analysis might reveal that a PRO was significantly impacted when popular composers moved their affiliations from one PRO to another.

So, if a sought-after composer creates some intro music for local morning news and he moves from ASCAP to SESAC, more local TV license fees should be flowing to SESAC and less to ASCAP to account for that change.

TVMLC uses a sampling approach (currently 200 stations, eight days of programming on each one). After the sample is selected, MRI and local TV stations identify as much of the music as possible, along with the current owners, their shares, and their PRO affiliations.

The Committee relies on stations to work with MRI, identifying the rightsholders and PRO affiliations for the music used in local programming. It requires stations to provide cue sheets for as much of their locally produced programming as possible. This music is generally not "popular." Instead, it is created by relatively unknown composers whose PRO affiliation should be identified, resulting in a market-share determination. The analysis should ultimately bring back royalty payments to those composers.

The Committee turns its data over to economists that use statistical techniques to calculate the amount of music use and PRO market shares for the industry.

Local radio works similarly to local TV with respect to music studies. In radio parlance, the market share of each PRO is referred to as the "spin share." Not surprisingly, several PROs believe that they have spin shares in local radio that collectively add up to more than 100%. The Radio Music License Committee also commissions and utilizes market-share studies in its negotiations with the PROs because of the lack of a reliable, public data source.

SECTION 10

SOUND RECORDINGS

Licensing requirements for sound recordings are quite different, depending on the type of media that's involved.

Performers bring the music and lyrics of musical works to life with sound recordings. And different media outlets that use music must follow very specific licensing regulations to share the recordings with the public.

> Under the copyright laws, musical works and sound recordings are considered separate works, with different legal rights and separate licensing schemes. They are generally owned and licensed separately. As a refresher -
>
> *Musical works* are compositions of music written by songwriters and composers. Songwriters and composers are often represented by music publishers.
>
> *Sound recordings* "fix" a unique rendition of that music in a tangible audio form. They are created by performers or recording artists who are often represented by record companies or "labels." Typically, the labels own the copyrights in the sound recordings and are responsible for promoting, distributing, and licensing sound recordings.

When a user needs licenses to both the musical work and the sound recording, the rights to these are typically secured separately. To make it even more complicated, the musical work may itself be owned jointly by multiple rightsholders. (Sound recordings can also be jointly owned, but this is far less common.)

Let's start with an example. Dolly Parton writes many of her own songs. Some of these songs—like "Jolene"—she records herself. Others—like "I Will Always Love You," made famous by Whitney Houston—are recorded by others.

> When a user needs licenses to both the musical work and the sound recording, the rights to these are typically secured separately.

Parton is a songwriter, in other words both a composer and lyricist, and has thus created a musical work—a copyrightable work of authorship. She has performed and recorded "Jolene," so she (or her record label) is also the holder of the sound recording rights—another copyrightable work of authorship.

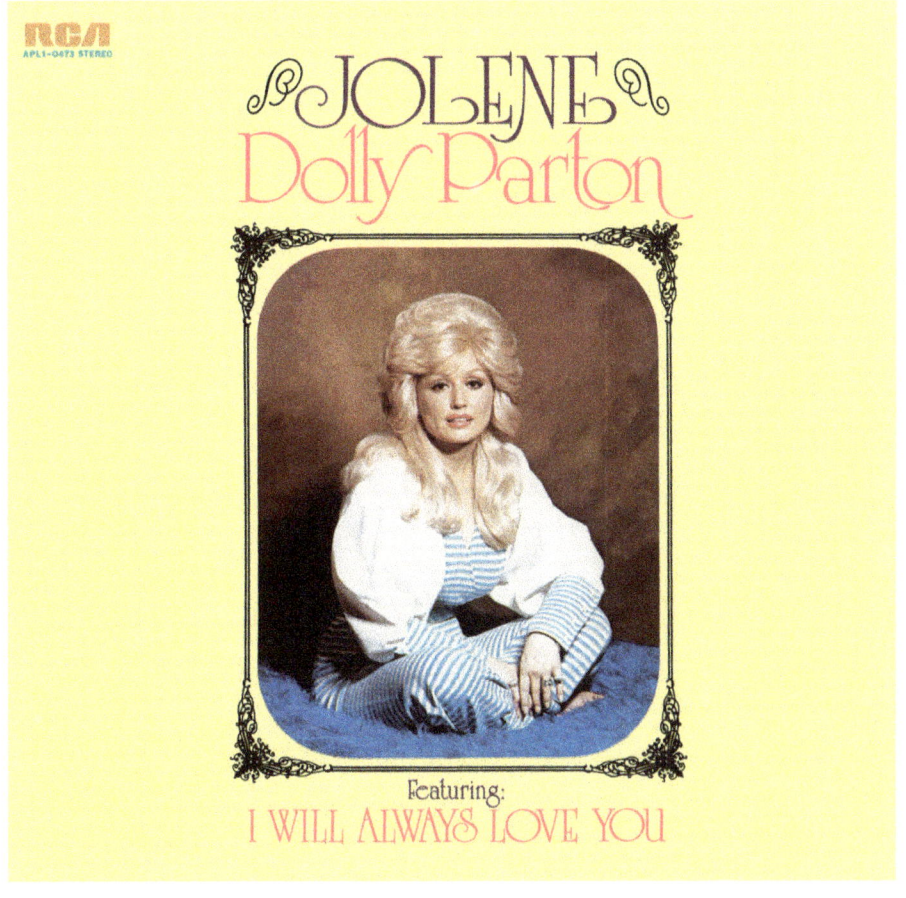

In exchange for ownership in the sound recording copyrights, her record label would typically create, market, promote, and license her sound recording of "Jolene." Because Parton wrote the song, she would receive royalty income from the licensing of the musical work as well as income from the sale and licensing of the sound recording.

Owners of sound recordings have a few different rights, under copyright laws. Let's look at each one in turn.

PUBLIC PERFORMANCE OF SOUND RECORDINGS—BROADCASTERS

The music and lyrics of much popular music are often not composed or written by the recording artist who made the music popular. Recording artists (even though they have not created a musical work) are entitled to royalties for certain uses of their sound recordings.

Only the owner of the copyright in the musical work has a general public performance right under the copyright laws. Owners of sound recordings do not have a general "exclusive right" to publicly perform their recordings. They only have the exclusive right to publicly perform the recording by means of a digital audio transmission.

> Owners of sound recordings do not have a general "exclusive right" to publicly perform their recordings. They only have the exclusive right to publicly perform the recording by means of a digital audio transmission.

The popularity of digital streaming services has made the public performance of sound recordings by digital audio transmission a very lucrative income source for recording artists and record labels.

The Digital Performance Rights in Sound Recording Act of 1995 (DPRSRA) is an amendment to the U.S. Copyright Act that created a limited performance right for sound recordings when they are transmitted by digital audio means. This right does not apply to the performance of audiovisual works such as TV programs or content developed by such outlets as Netflix. This Act also had no effect on local terrestrial radio stations (except to the extent the local radio station is also streaming its radio broadcast over the internet). In other words, over-the-air AM/FM radio does not need performance rights for sound recordings. But, if identical content is simulcast by the same radio station over the internet, then a sound recording performance rights license is required and royalties are owed (typically at rates set by the CRB).

> The bottom line is this: network and local TV do not need public performance licenses for sound recordings. Similarly, local broadcast radio (unless simulcast) does not need public performance licenses for sound recordings.

Although broadcasters need to pay royalties to composers and music publishers for the performance of musical works (the underlying compositions embedded in the sound recordings), they do not have to pay royalties for the right to perform sound recordings (i.e., specific audio versions of the musical compositions).

Following our example, broadcasters must pay Dolly Parton for the broadcast of "Jolene" (along with any other co-owners of the musical work via the PROs). But they don't need to pay her or her record label for sound recording performance rights.

If, however, TV broadcasters want to use a sound recording (like Dolly's version of "Jolene") in a pre-recorded program, then reproduction or "master use" rights are required. That's discussed in more detail later in this Section and in Section 12.

PUBLIC PERFORMANCE OF SOUND RECORDINGS—DIGITAL MUSIC

Interactive, digital streaming services like Apple Music, Amazon Music Unlimited, and Spotify clear the public performance rights for sound recordings through licenses negotiated directly with record labels. As noted in Section 6, they secure public performance rights for musical works in direct negotiations with music publishers and/or through the PROs. Fees are typically based on the number of service subscribers and/or the revenue of the service.

> Interactive, digital streaming services like Apple Music, Amazon Music Unlimited, and Spotify clear the public performance rights for sound recordings through licenses negotiated directly with record labels.

The circumstances are different for noninteractive services like Pandora's ad-supported service (the so-called "lean back" service), and satellite radio companies like Sirius XM. They don't need to negotiate with record labels for permission to publicly perform their sound recordings. Instead, they can clear public performance rights for sound recordings through statutory licenses under Section 114 of the Copyright Act.

Similarly, terrestrial radio stations that "simulcast" their broadcast signals over the internet may use the Section 114 statutory license.

To be eligible for the Section 114 statutory license, the music service must meet certain requirements. SoundExchange collects royalty payments under this statutory license, working on the behalf of sound recording copyright holders. The Copyright Royalty Board (CRB) determines the royalty rates and terms for the public performance of sound recordings pursuant to this statutory license. To date, the CRB has always set a fixed percentage of revenue rate or "per play" rate (depending on the type of music service) for this license which is paid to SoundExchange which compensates sound recording rightsholders and recording artists.

The Section 114 statutory license is only available to noninteractive services. To qualify, such services cannot allow the listener to select a particular song he or she wants to hear. Unlike the interactive services discussed earlier, these services do not offer "music on demand."

REPRODUCTION RIGHTS FOR SOUND RECORDINGS

The sound recordings owners also have rights of reproduction—the right to make copies of the sound recording (such as CDs or digital files). Generally, licenses to reproduce and distribute sound recordings necessary to transmit digital files or operate an interactive music service like Spotify are obtained through direct negotiations between the music service and sound recording owner, typically a record label, in a private, commercial transaction in the open market.

In the case of interactive services, the negotiation typically covers both the necessary sound recording performance and reproduction rights; a single license covers all the sound recording rights the service needs.

> The sound recordings owners also have rights of reproduction—the right to make copies of the sound recording (such as CDs or digital files).

There's a companion law to Section 114: Section 112, which covers certain sound recording reproduction rights. Section 112 creates a statutory license to enable noninteractive streaming services that perform sound recordings to make the necessary reproductions to facilitate the performance of the sound recording.

The statutory license under Section 114 applies to the public performance of sound recordings (see above), whereas the statutory license under Section 112 applies to a reproduction. Congress established this related statutory license under Section 112 to authorize the creation of these copies with rates and license terms also established by the CRB.

The rates and terms for the Section 112 and 114 licenses are established in the same rate-setting proceeding.

MASTER USE RIGHTS FOR SOUND RECORDINGS

Owners of sound recording rights also have master use rights—the sound recording right that is comparable to the musical works synchronization right. Section 12 is devoted to synchronization rights both for musical works and sound recordings.

A master use license allows for a particular sound recording to be combined with audiovisual works such as films and TV programs. This is like the musical works synchronization right. The fee structure for a master use license for sound recordings (like that for musical works synchronization rights) is typically negotiated in a private, commercial transaction, generally involving a flat fee.

Many TV stations get the necessary master use and synch licenses from music libraries. For popular music, these rights are typically secured from the record labels (for the master use rights) and publishers (for the synch rights).

RECAP–RIGHTS OF THE OWNERS OF SOUND RECORDINGS

Public performance rights (which do not involve the PROs who only license performance rights in musical works)

- Netflix, cable, network and local TV—no clearance required;
- Local terrestrial (over-the-air) radio—no clearance required;
- Internet radio (simulcast streaming of AM/FM radio)—statutory licenses can be obtained through Section 114;
- Digital, interactive streaming services—requires a license, typically directly from the record labels;
- Digital, noninteractive streaming services—statutory licenses can be obtained through Section 114.

Reproduction rights for audio-only services

- On-demand, digital interactive streaming services—voluntary licenses and direct negotiations with a record label (without statutory conditions), covering both reproduction rights and performance rights;
- Digital downloads—voluntary licenses and direct negotiations between a record label and digital service (without statutory conditions);
- Noninteractive digital streaming (including webcasters and satellite radio)—Section 114 statutory license is used for public performances, and Section 112 statutory license can be used to cover certain reproduction rights.

Master Use rights for audiovisual programs

- Netflix, cable, network, and local TV negotiate licenses privately with the record labels.

SECTION 11

REPRODUCTION AND DISTRIBUTION LICENSES

There are two possible avenues for obtaining reproduction and distribution rights: statutory licenses and negotiations with copyright holders. Which one is appropriate depends on specific circumstances.

Before diving into the topic of reproduction licenses for musical works and sound recordings, let's go over some of the information from previous sections.

Every recording has two parts that implicate different rights under the copyright laws: the composition, or musical work, and the sound recording. The composer and recording artist can be the same person, but frequently that is not the case. Even when they are the same person, the copyrights are typically owned by different companies, with a music publisher owning the musical work copyright and a record company owning the sound recording copyright.

> Composers and songwriters (and their publishers) earn royalties from their rights in the musical work. Recording artists (and their record label) earn royalties from their rights in the sound recording.

In addition to public performance rights, owners of musical works and sound recordings also control the right to reproduce their compositions or sound recordings.

> In addition to public performance rights, owners of musical works and sound recordings also control the right to reproduce their compositions or sound recordings.

For some musical work reproduction rights (so-called "mechanical rights"), there is a statutory license, with rates and terms determined by the Copyright Royalty Board (CRB). Historically, these mechanical rights were associated with the making of cassettes, CDs, and vinyl records.

Today, royalties for mechanical rights are also associated with on-demand streaming and digital downloads. Even though streaming and downloading are certainly not "mechanical", the historical term persists. Reproduction rights for musical works, to the extent needed by digital streaming services, are typically secured at a rate determined by the CRB.

> Reproduction rights for musical works, to the extent needed by digital streaming services, are typically secured at a rate determined by the CRB.

Other than the mechanical rights for musical works, reproduction rights licenses (such as for reproductions of sound recordings) are generally negotiated directly with the copyright holder.

HISTORY

While we have spent a good deal of time in this Guide on public performance rights, there are two other core rights of music copyright holders—for both musical works and sound recordings. They pertain to reproduction and distribution.

A reproduction right pertains to the duplication, transcription, imitation, or simulation of a work in fixed form. This right allows the copying of musical works (such as duplicating sheet music) or sound recordings (like CDs and digital downloads).

When someone holds distribution rights, a distinct right from reproduction rights, they can "distribute" (i.e., sell or provide) copies of a copyrighted work to the public.

Since the early days of copyright law, rightsholders in musical works—typically songwriters, composers, and publishers—have had the right to reproduce and distribute copies of their musical compositions. The word "mechanical" comes from the reproduction of music by piano rolls, which replaced the music box (for those who have no idea what a piano roll is).

The piano roll evolved into phonograph records (thanks to Thomas Edison), then CDs and, for the post-Millennials, digital downloads. All of these are still referred to as "mechanical reproductions," and musical works copyright owners have the right of reproduction.

Music and legal history buffs may recall a Supreme Court case called White Smith v. Apollo Music. The court ruled that piano rolls were not considered "copies," so there was no infringement of the composer's copyright.

Through legislation, Congress overturned White Smith in 1909 by granting to musical work copyright holders the right to control the mechanical reproduction of their works.

To limit the monopoly power of a single manufacturer of piano rolls, Congress created a "statutory" license for the licensing of mechanical rights for musical works.

In 1976, Congress codified the mechanical statutory license (for musical works) in Section 115 of the Copyright Act and determined that rates would be set by an administrative body now known as the CRB.

When record labels wish to make and distribute CDs or the resurgently popular vinyl albums, for example, they may obtain voluntary mechanical licenses directly from music publishers to cover the musical work underlying the sound recording. Alternatively, they may obtain a statutory license under Section 115 for purposes of securing the necessary musical works' mechanical rights.

> Although the Section 115 statutory license covers the musical work reproduction rights, it does not authorize the reproduction of a sound recording.

Permission to duplicate a sound recording, to the extent necessary, must be obtained from whomever owns the sound recording copyright—likely either the recording artist or record label.

ON-DEMAND STREAMING AND DIGITAL DOWNLOADS—REPRODUCTION AND DISTRIBUTION LICENSES—MUSICAL WORKS

As noted previously, digital interactive streaming services (also known as on-demand services) are required to secure both musical works public performance rights (as described in Section 6) and musical works "mechanical" (reproduction) rights. Their public performance rights for musical works are typically secured from PROs.

> On-demand services negotiate directly with record labels to clear sound recording reproduction rights. These negotiations typically cover both reproduction rights and performance rights for the sound recording.

To clear mechanical rights for musical works, interactive streaming services can take advantage of a statutory blanket license pursuant to Section 115 or get them directly from the music publishers. Noninteractive streaming services are not required to secure musical works mechanical rights.

The rates and terms for this statutory license are set either by negotiation between music publishers and songwriters (and their trade associations), on the one side, and the on-demand music streaming services, on the other, or, in the event of a negotiating impasse, by the Copyright Royalty Board (CRB).

Although Section 115 grants the necessary musical works mechanical rights licenses for digital downloads, the license does not authorize the reproduction or distribution of a sound recording. Those rights must be secured separately before making digital downloads available. Such rights are typically secured directly from record labels.

Section 115 was based on per-work or song-by-song licensing. Although this worked well for phonorecords and CDs, the efficiency of the system began to suffer as on-demand digital streaming became more and more popular.

The Music Modernization Act was designed to address, among other things, this issue and streamline the process, making it easier for rightsholders to get paid when their music is streamed by on-demand services. The MMA needs to be at the center of any discussion of mechanical reproduction licenses for musical works.

> The MMA needs to be at the center of any discussion of mechanical reproduction licenses for musical works.

THE MMA

According to the U.S. Copyright Office, the Orrin G. Hatch—Bob Goodlatte Music Modernization Act (the Music Modernization Act or MMA) is "the most significant piece of copyright legislation in decades and updates our current laws to reflect modern consumer preferences and technological developments in the music marketplace."

For this Guide, we will focus on Title 1 of the MMA. This title updates Section 115 by replacing song-by-song statutory licensing for making copies of and distributing musical works with blanket licensing. It applies to digital music providers that want to reproduce and distribute digital music downloads (offered by services like iTunes) or engage in interactive music streaming (like Spotify). The following is a verbatim (but shortened) description of key provisions of the MMA that can be found at www.copyright.gov.

Mechanical Licensing Collective

The legislation establishes a "mechanical licensing collective" ("MLC") to administer the blanket license, and a "digital licensee coordinator" ("DLC") to coordinate the activities of the licensees and designate a representative to serve as a non-voting member on the board of the MLC. The MLC will receive notices and reports from digital music providers, collect and distribute royalties, and identify musical works and their owners for payment. The MLC will establish and maintain a publicly accessible database containing information relating to musical works (and shares of such works) and, to the extent known, the identity and location of the copyright owners of such works and the sound recordings in which the musical works are embodied. In cases where the MLC is not able to match musical works to copyright owners, the MLC is authorized to distribute the unclaimed royalties to copyright owners identified in the MLC records, based on the relative market shares of such copyright owners as reflected in reports of usage provided by digital music providers for the periods in question.

The operational costs of the MLC will be paid for by digital music providers through voluntary contributions and an administrative assessment set by the Copyright Royalty Judges. The MLC and the DLC are authorized to participate in proceedings before the Copyright Royalty Judges to establish the administrative assessment.

Notices to Obtain License

The existing system for filing notices of intention to obtain a compulsory license for making and distributing phonorecords of nondramatic musical works ("NOIs") with the Copyright Office on a song-by-song basis will remain in place for non-digital uses (e.g., CDs, vinyl). However, the Office will no longer accept NOIs for making a digital phonorecord delivery of a musical work, such as in the form of a permanent download, limited download, or interactive stream. Instead, after a transition period, during which the Register will issue relevant regulations and designate key entities to carry out administration of the license, users will be able to obtain a blanket license (covering all musical works available for compulsory licensing) for digital phonorecord deliveries by submitting a notice of license to the MLC. While the Copyright Office will no longer accept NOIs for making a digital phonorecord delivery of musical works, licensees may still serve NOIs directly on copyright owners.

Interim Period

Prior to the license availability date (January 1, 2021), liability may be limited to royalties due under the compulsory license if the digital music provider complies with certain requirements, including engaging in good-faith, commercially reasonable efforts to identify and locate each copyright owner of a musical work they use on their service.

Rate Standard

The new rate-setting standard applied by the Copyright Royalty Judges will be a market-based willing buyer / willing seller standard, replacing the policy-oriented 801(b)(1) rate-setting standard.

Important Note - *A mechanical license for musical works for interactive streaming may be either obtained through a voluntary license from a music publisher or through a blanket license from the mechanical licensing collective pursuant to the MMA.*

NONINTERACTIVE STREAMING-REPRODUCTION LICENSES-SOUND RECORDINGS

Audiences continue to consume music through means other than interactive streaming services such as Spotify. Radio stations still simulcast over the internet, and satellite radio is still an option. There are "custom" internet radio services such as that offered by Pandora.

> Remember—noninteractive services and simulcasters, satellite radio, and over-the-air radio broadcasters are not obligated to secure musical works mechanical rights licenses.

Noninteractive services make server reproductions of sound recordings to facilitate digital transmissions. Recognizing this, Congress established a related statutory license under Section 112 to authorize the creation of these copies. Rates and terms for these reproductions are established by the CRB with payment and reporting of royalties made to SoundExchange. On-demand digital music streaming services like Spotify do not qualify for the Section 112 statutory license—they secure any necessary sound recording reproduction rights directly from record labels.

SECTION 12

SYNCHRONIZATION RIGHTS

Obtaining synch rights is half the battle when clearing music rights for video productions. Here's the nitty-gritty.

If you've been reading sections of this Guide sequentially, then you probably recall how I've stressed that it's generally not enough to just clear performance rights for musical works (through the PROs) to broadcast audiovisual content containing music.

A synchronization license is also typically needed for movies, TV shows, and other types of pre-recorded audiovisual content. Synchronization licenses are required for the musical work and so-called "master use" rights licenses are needed if using a pre-existing sound recording.

First, here are some basic definitions:

Section 101 of the Copyright Act defines **audiovisual works** as "works that consist of a series of related images which are intrinsically intended to be shown by the use of machines, or devices such as projectors, viewers, or electronic equipment, together with accompanying sounds, if any, regardless of the nature of the material objects, such as films or

> A synchronization license is also typically needed for movies, TV shows, and other types of pre-recorded audiovisual content. Synchronization licenses are required for the musical work and so-called "master use" rights licenses are needed if using a pre-existing sound recording.

tapes, in which the works are embodied." Some examples include motion pictures, television programs, and music videos.

A *synchronization license* is one that permits the licensee to incorporate a musical work into an audiovisual work such as a motion picture or television program and to then make copies of the audiovisual works that contain the licensed music, pursuant to the terms specified in the license.

Synchronization or *synch* occurs when a producer uses music in timed relation with video. The copyright law does not explicitly mention synchronization rights, but these rights are generally understood to be derived from the musical works rightsholder's reproduction and/or derivative works rights.

Synch licenses are negotiated in private, commercial transactions, typically for a flat fee. They are not subject to or affected by statutory licenses or consent decrees.

TV producers and movie producers typically face different regulatory hurdles when clearing synch and performance rights. It's a more streamlined process for the film industry. Movie theaters do not get public performance licenses from the PROs covering the music in the movies. Instead, producers clear those rights with the copyright owners when they clear synchronization rights. Thus, movie producers clear both their public performance rights and synch rights at the same time from the same source. Unfortunately, TV producers generally do not use this same efficient licensing method as the producers do not secure the public performance rights. That is left to the broadcaster or the media outlet.

> Productions for TV—whether produced locally, by networks, or by syndicators—must clear both synchronization rights and public performance rights.

Productions for TV—whether produced locally, by networks, or by syndicators—must clear both synchronization rights and public performance rights. They must do this for all kinds of music usage–from music themes for newscasts to the background for local lifestyle and sports shows to bumpers and promotional content. The list goes on.

While for TV, public performance rights are typically negotiated with the PROs, synch licenses for locally produced TV programs are generally obtained from commercial music libraries such as Warner Chappell, Killer Tracks, and many others. In other words, the synch rights to the music are cleared through third parties that have all the rights to license the music for these purposes.

> While for TV, public performance rights are typically negotiated with the PROs, synch licenses for locally produced TV programs are generally obtained from commercial music libraries.

The use of popular music in audiovisual productions can be a costly proposition—the synch rights for popular music are generally more expensive than those for lesser-known works. For that reason, local TV typically does not use popular music in its locally produced programs or commercials. Music libraries offer more affordable options: compositions that are not well known.

MASTER USE LICENSES

We talked briefly about master use licenses in Section 10 on Sound Recordings.

To use an actual pre-existing recording—think Bruce Springsteen singing "Born in the USA" or Pharrell Williams singing "Happy"—a producer must also obtain a "master use license." This is a type of license that covers the sound recording being used in the program.

A master use license is an agreement between the owner of the sound recording and the content producer for the use of a particular sound recording in the production. It is obtained from the person who owns the sound recording rights (generally the record label) and is typically required for many kinds of productions, ranging from pre-recorded local TV shows to content on giant streaming services like Netflix or commercials for brands like Toyota.

> TV stations should never forget about obtaining the proper synch rights for any video productions using music.

It is a common misconception that TV stations' licenses from the PROs (which come at a significant cost particularly for a small market station) are all that is needed to secure the right to air music in local programming. TV stations should never forget about obtaining the proper synch rights for any video productions using music.

A VERY LIMITED EXCEPTION: "EPHEMERAL USE"

The word "ephemeral" means something that is temporary or momentary—lasting for a very short time period. The statutory provision of the copyright law that relates to ephemeral uses of sound recordings can be found in 17 U.S.C. Section 112.

There is a limited ephemeral use exception for broadcasters that usually applies to a live transmission such as a live newscast or sporting event.

This exception applies only to the initial broadcast of a program. Any rebroadcasts or other repurposing of the original content likely requires a license for the use of the music. The exemption applies only to broadcasters (not to studios, production houses, or other entities). And it might not apply in cases where pre-produced content is incorporated into a live broadcast.

If the exception applies—and we strongly suggest that you consult counsel as to whether the ephemeral use exception applies—no master use rights/licenses are required.

QUESTIONS FROM OUR AUDIENCE

Q: I work at a TV station and want to produce a commercial using some popular music. I also want to use popular music in bumps for my morning news. We have licenses from all of the PROs. Am I covered?

A: No. To incorporate music into an audiovisual work—such as a film or television program—the creator of that audiovisual work generally must obtain both 1) synchronization licenses from the owner of the musical work and 2) a master use license from the owner of the sound recording (if using a pre-existing recording). Your PRO licenses likely grant your station the right to publicly perform the music in the commercial and morning news programs (so long as that music is in the repertory of one of the PROs with which you have a license). But PRO licenses do not provide the rights necessary to actually incorporate that music into the program. Synchronization licenses are usually obtained from music publishers while master use licenses are typically obtained from record labels. If you are not using popular music, you may be able to get all the rights you need from music libraries such as Killer Tracks. If you do purchase music from a music library, you will want to ensure that the purchase includes a grant of both synchronization and master use rights, and explicitly covers both the musical work and the sound recording – and that the music library offers indemnification if there is any claim of infringement based on your licensed use of the purchased music.

SECTION 13

JUDICIAL AND LEGISLATIVE HISTORY

A historical timeline and key court case summaries provide an overview of music licensing's legal underpinnings as they developed through the years.

This Guide is not meant to be a treatise or historical review of the copyright laws. Nor is it intended to be an exhaustive look at judicial history. But the brief history that follows shows how particular court cases and the development of the U.S. Copyright Act have profoundly shaped how broadcasters and others pay music creators and their representatives.

If the list of critical dates and the summary of key court cases whets your appetite for a deeper understanding, check out the resources at the end of this Guide. They provide excellent historical background.

KEY DATES—U.S. COPYRIGHT ACT

1814 The dawn of music publishing in the United States—in my hometown of Baltimore, Maryland—began when Francis Scott Key wrote our national anthem, "The Star-Spangled Banner." He created his passionate song after the British burned the Capitol, the Library of Congress, and the White House during the War of 1812.

1897 Congress grants musical works owners the exclusive right to perform their works publicly.

1909 The Copyright Act recognizes musical work copyright owners' exclusive right to make and distribute phonorecords—in other words, mechanical reproductions of musical works. This right is subject to a statutory license and continues today. See 1976 below. No copyright is yet extended to the sound recordings themselves.

1941 To resolve antitrust lawsuits brought by the U.S. Department of Justice against ASCAP, the two entities entered into a consent decree that prevents ASCAP from fully exploiting its market power. BMI and the DOJ also entered into a consent decree in the same year to resolve similar concerns. Both the ASCAP and BMI decrees have since been amended: BMI's most recently in 1994 and ASCAP's most recently in 2001.

1972 Congress recognizes artists' sound recordings as a distinct class of copyrighted work.

1976 Congress recodifies the statutory license for mechanical rights for musical works in the Copyright Act's Section 115 and creates an administrative tribunal to set rates. The tribunal is a predecessor to today's Copyright Royalty Board (CRB).

> **1995** Congress enacts the Digital Performance Right in Sound Recordings Act. This expanded Section 115 (mechanical rights for musical works) to cover digital transmissions of music. It also granted sound recording owners a limited public performance right for digital audio transmissions. However, certain sound recording performance rights are subject to statutory licensing under Sections 112 and 114 of the Copyright Act as described in Section 10.
>
> **2008/ 2009** Interactive streaming services first utilize the Section 115 statutory licensing rate-setting process to cover musical work reproduction rights (mechanical rights) to facilitate streaming.
>
> **2018** Congress passes the Music Modernization Act.

KEY COURT CASES

***Alden-Rochelle Inc. v. ASCAP*, 80 F. Supp. 888 (S.D.N.Y. 1948)**—This 1940s court case was an early challenge to the legality of certain ASCAP licensing practices. The court evaluated whether ASCAP violated antitrust laws when it prohibited its members from granting public performance rights, along with synchronization (synch) rights, to motion picture producers. At issue was ASCAP's requirement that movie theaters sign blanket license agreements for public performances if they wanted to show motion pictures to audiences.

At the time, movie producers were already negotiating with the actual rightsholders for the necessary synch rights. If it wasn't for this ASCAP practice, they could have also secured the necessary public performance rights as part of the same transaction (and before the music was incorporated into the movie).

ASCAP was able to seek and secure rate hikes because the negotiations for public performance rights took place after the music was already embedded in the motion pictures. And theaters were unable to choose among competing sources of music. The court ultimately concluded that ASCAP's practice violated the antitrust laws.

After Alden-Rochelle, ASCAP's consent decree was amended to eliminate this practice, but the amendment was limited to motion pictures shown in movie theaters. It does not apply more broadly to other audio-visual programming (or even to movies that are shown on television).

United States v. ASCAP (In Re Application of Buffalo Broad. Co.), No. 13-95 (WCC), 1993 WL 60687 (S.D.N.Y. Mar. 1, 1993)—The TVMLC scored its first significant success in moving toward its goal of competitive market rates when a rate court decided against ASCAP in a 1993 rate court proceeding.

In the case (commonly referred to as the Buffalo Broadcasting decision), the local television industry successfully moved away from paying ASCAP on a percentage-of-revenue basis, instead paying flat fees. In that same decision, the local television industry secured, for the first time, a meaningful alternative to the traditional "all or nothing" blanket license. (For more on this, see Section 8 and references to local TV's "per program" license throughout this Guide.)

SESAC and TVMLC (Meredith Corp., et al. v. SESAC, LLC, 1 F.Supp.3d 180 (S.D.N.Y. 2014))—SESAC, the third major U.S. PRO, is not subject to a consent decree with the Department of Justice, yet virtually every local broadcaster requires a license from SESAC. Because of the immense leverage that gave SESAC during negotiations, three broadcasters filed a class action suit in December 2009. The trio—Meredith Broadcasting, Scripps-Howard Broadcasting, and Hoak Media (since purchased by Gray Television) received legal funding from the TVMLC.

The antitrust lawsuit alleged that SESAC's licensing practices violated Sections 1 and 2 of the Sherman Act. The local TV industry was able to reach a settlement after more than five years of litigation, $16 million in legal costs, and defeating SESAC's motion to dismiss and a motion for summary judgment. In addition to significant monetary relief, SESAC agreed to certain restraints, limiting its ability to exploit its market power fully.

In February 2015, the court overseeing the lawsuit approved the settlement, which covers the period 2016-2035. The settlement provides local stations with many of the protections found in the ASCAP and BMI consent decrees. For example, SESAC can't launch copyright infringement lawsuits while license fees and terms are being negotiated. SESAC was also required to offer a meaningful per program license, beginning in 2016.

Although the settlement does not include the federal court determinations of reasonable fees, it does establish the right to binding arbitration if TVMLC and SESAC cannot agree on license fees and terms. Fees specified in arbitration are binding for four-year periods.

For more information about a similar history between the RMLC and SESAC, see Section 7.

Partial Withdrawal Cases—Legal challenges arose when some of the largest music publishers sought to license their public performance rights in two ways. For most users, the publishers licensed their works through the PROs, but for others (the large digital streaming services), the publishers sought to license their works directly with the service outside of the purview of the ASCAP and BMI consent decrees.

This practice, which came to be known as "partial" or "selective" withdrawal, was challenged by Pandora in two different rate court proceedings: one against ASCAP and the other against BMI. The judges overseeing the litigations both concluded that the ASCAP and BMI consent decrees did not allow for partial withdrawals.

In the ASCAP proceeding, Judge Denise Cote concluded that if a right-sholder wants to license its rights to some music users through ASCAP, it must license its rights to all music users through ASCAP. (In other words, if you're in for one, you're in for all.)

Judge Louis Stanton, who was overseeing the BMI litigation, had a different take. He concluded that if a rightsholder wants to license its rights to certain music users outside of the purview of the BMI consent decree, that rightsholder cannot license any music user through BMI. (If you're out for one, you're out for all).

Fractional Licensing—In 2016, the Department of Justice (DOJ) concluded that BMI and ASCAP should not be allowed to engage in fractional licensing (instead of licensing whole works). After an extensive review, the DOJ concluded that this was not in the public interest.

Almost immediately after that, BMI went to the court overseeing its consent decree and sought a ruling that the decree does not prohibit fractional licensing. The district court agreed with BMI.

The issue was then appealed to the Second Circuit, which ruled that the BMI decree doesn't specifically address fractional licensing; it is silent in that regard. Therefore, the court concluded that the language of the BMI decree does not prohibit fractional licensing.

The Second Circuit did not explicitly consider the merits of the public interest analysis undergirding the DOJ's prior evaluation. Instead, the court stated that if fractional licensing raises unresolved competitive concerns, the DOJ should move to amend the consent decrees, prohibiting such practices expressly. The DOJ has yet to take the Second Circuit up on this invitation.

In Section 16, we discuss the above topics in more detail.

SECTION 14

THE CONSENT DECREES

Two separate Department of Justice investigations have focused on whether regulations to rein in the market power of ASCAP and BMI should remain in place.

SUMMARY

ASCAP and BMI collectively control approximately 90% of U.S. performing rights, according to some reports, although the percentage of performance rights controlled by ASCAP and BMI varies for each type of licensee. Music is performed publicly in restaurants and bars as well as on mass media outlets like TV, radio, and music streaming services.

ASCAP and BMI take all their music and bundle it into a single license. In other words, music users cannot get a license covering just the works they want to play. It's also unrealistic for most users to secure licenses for all the works they play directly from songwriters and publishers.

For TV stations, along with users like Netflix, programming is frequently received with "music in the can." As a result, they have no control over the music played. Moreover, these outlets can't always determine what music is actually performed.

> Several years ago, the DOJ looked at several aspects of the consent decrees at the request of ASCAP and BMI. After exhaustive investigation, it concluded, "the current system has well served music creators and music users for decades and should remain intact."

The "take it or leave it" aspect of these licenses (with the "leave it" option likely to result in potentially crippling copyright infringement lawsuits) gives ASCAP and BMI enormous market power. Because of that, the Department of Justice (DOJ) brought antitrust lawsuits against them decades ago. These lawsuits were resolved with the imposition of "consent decrees", a type of regulation that reigned in this market power to some degree.

The decrees allowed for the negotiation of more reasonable license fees. And they provided limited government oversight of the PROs, which included the establishment of a "rate court." It is tasked with setting "reasonable" fees if a music user and either ASCAP or BMI cannot reach an agreement on license fees and terms.

The decrees also affect the two PROs in other ways. For example, they are required to give music users automatic licenses on request, providing music users with protection from copyright infringement concerns while negotiations over license fees and terms are ongoing.

Several years ago, the DOJ looked at several aspects of the consent decrees at the request of ASCAP and BMI. After exhaustive investigation, it concluded, "the current system has well served music creators and music users for decades and should remain intact." The consent decrees continue to provide a check on potential anticompetitive behavior.

HISTORY

Federal copyright law has long recognized copyright owners' right to control their musical works' public performance. In 1914, a group of composers and publishers formed ASCAP to enforce their performance rights and create a joint pool of musical compositions that could be licensed in bulk to music users. After that, ASCAP created the so-called "blanket" license that gave the user the ability to perform any musical composition within its entire repertory by paying a single license fee.

Since ASCAP was the only U.S. PRO at that time, its members had significant control over who could profit by writing music for public performance. And since ASCAP was the only significant music source, it had tremendous leverage in licensing negotiations with users. ASCAP's aggressive use of this leverage led the DOJ to commence antitrust actions against it beginning in the 1930s.

In 1941, the DOJ sued ASCAP again for violations of the Sherman Antitrust Act. The result was a voluntary consent decree in which ASCAP agreed to certain restrictions on its operations that affect its relationships with composers and publishers as well as music users. In the same year, BMI signed a similar consent decree. The DOJ amended the ASCAP consent decree in 1950. The most notable change was the establishment of a "rate court" giving both ASCAP and the music user the right to ask a court to set "reasonable" fees for ASCAP licenses if the parties involved in a negotiation did not come to an agreement.

Further revisions to the ASCAP consent decree occurred in 2001. The BMI consent decree was last amended in 1994, at which point a BMI "rate court" was also established.

THE RULES
Under the consent decrees, ASCAP and BMI:

1. Must issue licenses (or interim licenses) on request even if negotiations are still ongoing. If this regulation had not been established, the PROs could threaten music users with copyright infringement lawsuits as a negotiating tactic to extract unreasonable fees.

2. Must offer economically viable alternatives to a fixed-fee blanket license. For local TV broadcasters, these mandated alternatives include a per program license. This has enabled stations to secure public performance rights for at least some of the music they use in competitive transactions made directly with rightsholders (or via producer source licensing) without having to pay twice for those rights—once directly to the rightsholder and then again to ASCAP or BMI.

3. Cannot prevent their member composers and publishers from dealing directly with music users, including TV stations. As a result, individual copyright holders can potentially compete against each other on price and other terms.

4. Must offer comparable licenses to "similarly situated" entities preventing price discrimination.

5. Are subject to judicial oversight regarding the terms on which they license the right to perform the songs in their repertories. More specifically, the consent decrees empower the Federal District Court for the Southern District of New York to act as "rate court" in setting "reasonable" license fees if negotiations between the parties break down and one of the parties requests judicial intervention. In doing so, the rate court is tasked with setting fees that most closely resemble those that would result from a competitive marketplace. Many music users, including radio and TV, have periodically resorted to rate court relief because of unreasonable fee demands from ASCAP and BMI.

MUSIC INDUSTRY CRITICISM

ASCAP and BMI have criticized this system and the continuation of the consent decrees. One point of contention relates to a section of the ASCAP consent decree that restricts it from offering synch licenses. It can only offer public performance licenses. As noted in Section 12, synch licenses allow musical compositions to be used in audiovisual works, a lucrative royalty source.

Moreover, ASCAP cannot offer mechanical licenses. As discussed in Section 11, mechanical licenses relate to a separate musical works right that is needed, for example, by interactive streaming services such as Spotify. BMI's consent decree is worded differently and does not explicitly prohibit BMI from licensing mechanical rights. But BMI has not expanded its offerings beyond public performance rights licensing.

Another bone of contention relates to smaller PROs, including SESAC and GMR, which are not subject to consent decrees. ASCAP and BMI contend that they are at a competitive disadvantage because their rivals are unregulated.

Music publishers have their own problems with the consent decrees. For more on that, visit Section 16, which discusses "selective withdrawals."

RECENT DOJ REVIEW—ROUND 1

The DOJ looked at several aspects of the consent decrees at the request of ASCAP and BMI and conducted an exhaustive investigation that began in 2014. As a result of that review, DOJ concluded that the consent decrees continue to serve the public interest by mitigating the monopoly power created through collective licensing.

That comprehensive multi-year review included two rounds of public comments. Over 330 sets of comments were provided, and there were dozens of meetings between the DOJ's Antitrust Division and industry stakeholders.

The DOJ division issued a closing statement on August 4, 2016. (It's formally known as the Statement of the Department of Justice on the Closing of the Antitrust Division's Review of the ASCAP and BMI Consent Decrees.) After its thorough investigation, the DOJ "decided not to seek to modify the decrees." It concluded that the "current system has well served music creators and music users for decades and should remain intact."

RECENT DOJ REVIEW—ROUND 2

On June 5, 2019, the DOJ announced that it had once again opened a review of the ASCAP and BMI consent decrees—the second review of the decrees undertaken by the DOJ within five years. This time, the DOJ sought to determine whether the decrees should be maintained in their current form, modified, or terminated.

At that time, the ASCAP and BMI consent decrees were among 1,300 "legacy" judgments overseen by DOJ's Antitrust Division. The year before the review began, in the spring of 2018, the Division decided to review many of these judgments to make sure "they're not doing more harm than good," in the words of its head, (now former) Assistant Attorney General Makan Delrahim. In fact, he called them "a mess" during a speech at Vanderbilt Law School on March 27, 2018.

"The ASCAP and BMI decrees have been in existence in some form for over seventy-five years and have effectively regulated how musicians are compensated for the public performance of their musical creations," said Delrahim. "There have been many changes in the music industry during this time, and the needs of music creators and music users have continued to evolve. It is important for the Division to reassess periodically whether these decrees continue to serve the American consumer and whether they should be changed to achieve greater efficiency and enhance competition in light of innovations in the industry."

The TVMLC and many other music users filed comments with the DOJ, as did ASCAP, BMI, music publishers, and songwriters. In August 2019, the DOJ received over 800 comments in response to its review.

As noted previously, in addition to TV and radio, music users affected by a possible termination of the consent decrees include bars, restaurants, hotels, and digital music services, to name a few. While many music users regarded the consent decrees as an "imperfect" solution to reining in the monopoly power of ASCAP and BMI, they were alarmed by the DOJ's proposal that the decrees might no longer be "relevant."

This was even more surprising because three years before, the DOJ had, as noted above, concluded that the decrees served a useful purpose and should remain intact.

Before long, Congress became concerned that ASCAP and BMI would be able to charge exorbitant fees to the music-user community if the consent decrees were amended or terminated. In a letter to Delrahim on June 8, 2018, leaders of the Senate and House Judiciary Committees noted that ASCAP and BMI "collectively license over 90 percent of musical works to licensees that publicly perform music, including restaurants, retail stores, bars, radio and TV broadcasters, and digital music services."

The letter stated: "The ASCAP and BMI decrees have been in place since the 1940s and reflect antitrust concerns arising from an entity collectively licensing works from competitors and offering them at a single price. While there are differing opinions on the substance of the ASCAP and BMI decrees, it is obvious that the marketplace for licensing public performance rights in musical works has been shaped for decades by these decrees. Terminating them without a clear alternative framework in place would result in a serious disruption in the marketplace, harming creators, copyright owners, licensees, and consumers."

IMPACT OF THE MUSIC MODERNIZATION ACT

In June of 2018, the Music Modernization Act (MMA) won the Senate Judiciary Committee's unanimous approval, paving the way for a full

Senate vote on the bill. The House version of the bill passed unanimously, and the bill was signed into law on October 18, 2018. The bill was designed, in part, to address developments related to the digital music age and is discussed in more detail in Section 11.

The MMA was not designed to address music performance rights in TV and radio. But it includes a provision that requires the DOJ to consult with Congress before filing a motion to terminate an ASCAP/BMI consent decree and notify Congress at least 90 days before it takes any steps in federal court to terminate the decrees.

COMMENTARY

As a part of its most recent review of the consent decrees, the DOJ requested comments on some critical questions. For example, do the consent decrees continue to serve important competitive purposes today? And would termination of the consent decrees serve the public interest? TVMLC and many others believe strongly that the answer to the first question is yes and the answer to the second is no.

The consent decrees remain as valuable and necessary today as they were when first put in place. Copyrighted music is still publicly performed. If it is played without a license, the user is subject to copyright infringement claims. ASCAP and BMI still control the vast majority of public performance rights in musical works and wield massive market power. It's almost impossible to operate a TV or radio station without taking a license from both PROs.

Recent TV and radio settlements with SESAC support the continuing need for the consent decrees. In 2014, a New York federal district judge sided with plaintiffs in a class action lawsuit brought on behalf of the local television industry. The judge determined that the evidence presented during discovery could clearly support a finding that SESAC had engaged in anticompetitive conduct, failed to offer a meaningful per program license, and possessed monopoly power, giving it the ability to control prices.

SESAC settled the litigation resulting in a refund of tens of millions of dollars to the industry. SESAC now operates similarly to ASCAP and BMI in its dealing with local TV. For example, it offers licenses on request; is subject to a neutral rate-setting mechanism in the event of negotiation impasse; and offers a meaningful per program license to local TV stations. SESAC also settled similar litigation with the radio industry.

"The consent decrees have benefited both purveyors of music and the listening public, and so we're not standing in line and saying let's get rid of them," said Dennis Wharton, (now former) executive vice president of the National Association of Broadcasters.

Music streaming services, simulcasters and webcasters agree. The Digital Media Association has said that the consent decrees continue to provide a check on potential anticompetitive behavior.

What would happen if the consent decrees were lifted? Would the PROs increase license fees? Eliminate per program licenses? Prevent users from negotiating directly with publishers and composers?

How would music users react? Engage in costly, private antitrust litigation?

"The ASCAP and BMI Consent Decrees were originally established to guard against anticompetitive behavior and we have seen no evidence that they have outlived their intended purpose. If anything, they are more critical than ever in an increasingly complex and diverse licensing environment which, without measures that ensure an orderly market, is ripe for abuse," said the MIC Coalition, a group of associations whose members provide music in venues and over the airwaves.

"Modifying the existing decrees for the sake of change, alone, will not lead to the advent of a new and improved licensing regime that yields greater competition or adequately protects consumer interests," they added.

DOJ—ROUND 2 CONCLUSION

In January 2021, one day before Delrahim stepped down from his position at the DOJ, he returned to Vanderbilt Law School to hold a webinar on the consent decree investigation results. The conclusion was the same as in 2016. The DOJ would leave in place the pair of decrees that have regulated the behavior of ASCAP and BMI for nearly 80 years.

Delrahim indicated that not enough consensus existed between music users and purveyors to change, sunset, or terminate them. Delrahim said the review showed that disagreements continue to exist among songwriters and others in the music community about the "benefits, drawbacks and continued need" for the decrees. But in the end, he said, termination was not an option in the short term because the industry still relies on them.

Instead, "Continued review of, and stakeholder input concerning, the decrees remain necessary to ensure the decrees continue to satisfy their purpose to protect competition and do not act as an impediment to innovation," Delrahim added.

For the second time in the last five years, the DOJ has determined that the consent decrees—while perhaps controversial—are still necessary to, among other things, protect music users from ASCAP and BMI charging unreasonable license fees.

SECTION 15

FAIR USE AND RELATED TOPICS

The term "fair use" is sometimes thrown around as a way to air music for which proper licensing has not been obtained. Know the rules and tread with care.

To save time and avoid license fees, music users are always looking for ways to find exceptions to copyright laws. Some undertakings of this type are wise and legitimate, while others need to be carefully scrutinized by legal counsel. In this section, we look at some circumstances where licenses might not be required or can be obtained at a reduced fee.

Create or Buy It Yourself—Broadcasters and other content producers sometimes engage a composer to write music exclusively for its programming. This type of work is considered "a work for hire," which means that the company commissioning the work owns all rights to that music, as long as a written agreement specifies that the work will be produced as a work for hire.

Similarly, if an employee composes music for a program within the scope of their employment, the employer owns that music's rights, even without a separate written agreement. The company can then use the musical compositions in perpetuity without additional payment to the original creator.

Music bought outright in the open market or created as a "work for hire" can be used by the broadcaster in any way it wants—from intros, background music, and bumps to locally produced programming and advertising. No synch rights licenses or public performance licenses are needed for that music.

Many large TV broadcasters buy music in the open market. They own their own news themes and other music used in local programming. ESPN, for example, owns much of the music that it uses in the programming it produces. Similarly, many local TV broadcasters buy outright the synchronization and public performance rights to the music used in their locally produced programming, such as news.

Broadcasters still need synch rights and performance rights for non-owned music. But outright ownership of music (along with the purchase of performance rights from music libraries) allows stations to reduce their license fee obligations to the PROs if they utilize the per program license or other alternatives to the fixed-fee blanket license. As noted in Section 8, per program licenses can reduce fees paid to the PROs.

Copyright Expiration — There are legal limits placed on a copyright owner's control over how their works are used. If, for example, the period of exclusivity provided by copyright law has expired, then the work has entered the "public domain" and is freely available for use without a license. The duration of copyright protection is long - for works recently created, it generally extends for the life of the creator plus 70 years.

Public Domain—The failure of a work to provide a copyright notice, that is, to contain on its face a claim of copyright protection, is not a reliable basis for concluding that a work is in the public domain. Unfortunately, there is no government-compiled list or other authoritative source that identifies public domain music. While not bullet-proof, some websites offer listings of public domain music. You can also check the PRO websites to try and determine whether a particular song you want to use is in the public domain.

One must be careful, however, because each country has a different scheme to protect intellectual property. A song that has fallen in the public domain in the United States might still be protected in other countries.

Much of the music from the World War I era has fallen into the public domain. However, suppose an old song is incorporated with a different arrangement or orchestration into a popular song. In that case, that song might be copyrighted more recently and considered a new work with a separate copyright duration.

> **Much patriotic, historical, and religious music is now in the public domain. Here are some examples:**
>
> "Oh! Susanna" by Stephen Collins Foster
>
> "Dixie" by Daniel Emmett
>
> "Maryland, My Maryland" by James Ryder Randall
>
> "America the Beautiful" by Katherine Lee Bates and Samuel A. Ward
>
> "Stars and Stripes Forever" (and almost everything by John Philip Sousa)
>
> "You're a Grand Old Flag" by George M. Cohan
>
> "Danny Boy" by Frederic E. Weatherly

Fair Use — Certain uses of copyrighted material constitute "fair use." These are uses that are viewed as either so inconsequential or so important in terms of news or educational value that the works are legally usable for certain purposes without the copyright holder's consent. Determinations are made case by case and are very fact-specific.

Reliance on fair use as the basis for not seeking permission for use is not recommended without the advice of legal counsel.

Fair use is an affirmative defense to a claim of copyright infringement. Affirmative defenses are typically not decided until the litigation of a case is complete. Consequently, reliance on such defenses carries risk, particularly if the goal is to avoid litigation as well as liability.

Section 107 of the Copyright Act codifies the fair use doctrine. It states that copyrighted content can be used free of license for "criticism, comment, news reporting, teaching ... scholarship, or research...."

Various factors are weighed to determine if a particular use is a "fair use," including, according to the copyright laws:

1. The purpose and character of the use, including whether such use is of a commercial nature or is for nonprofit educational purposes;
2. The nature of the copyrighted work;
3. The amount and substantiality of the portion used in relation to the copyrighted work as a whole; and
4. The effect of the use upon the potential market for, or value of, the copyrighted work.

These factors have generated considerable litigation. In the end, whether something is deemed "fair use" is extremely fact-driven.

On one end of the spectrum is the use of sheet music in an elementary school music class or the playing of music for sight-challenged students to assist with hearing and speech. These types of uses have been deemed as fair uses with no obligation to copyright holders. For other uses, the courts have had a field day.

It pays to take a look at some of the more interesting and important cases:

- Lennon v. Premise Media Corp., 556 F. Supp. 2d 310 (S.D.N.Y. 2008) was brought by John Lennon's widow and children against the producer of a documentary. The film, which is about the theory of evolution, included a 15-second excerpt of the song "Imagine." On screen, the following words appeared: "Nothing to kill or die for/ And no religion too." Like most fair use cases, the case has many moving parts and contains a careful assessment of the facts. But bottom line: since this was a documentary including interviews with folks who had doubts about religion, the court concluded that the song and lyrics' limited use fell into the category of "criticism and commentary."

- One of the most important fair use cases for TV broadcasters is Italian Book Corp. v. American Broadcasting Companies, 458 Supp. 65 (S.D.N.Y. 1978). A court determined that there was no copyright infringement when ABC News televised a parade during which the plaintiff's copyrighted music was played. The use at issue did not result in any damage to the composer or the market for the composer's work. That finding was one of the key reasons why the court reached its decision.

- Many interesting cases involve comedic parodies. Among the more salacious is Elsmere Music, Inc. v. National Broadcasting Co., 623 F.2d 252 (2d Cir. 1980). The court held that it was fair use for "Saturday Night Live" to use the song "I Love New York," retitling it "I Love Sodom" and replacing the words with some irreverent lyrics.

- Another significant case was decided on March 7, 1994, by the U.S. Supreme Court. It held that the copyright to the song "Oh, Pretty Woman" by Roy Orbison and William Dees may not have been infringed by a very different song entitled "Pretty Woman," recorded by the hip hop group 2 Live Crew. I'll leave the lyrics to your imagination, but the court delved into an excellent analysis of the four-factor test noted above. If you are interested in knowing more, read the case: Campbell v. Acuff-Rose Music, Inc., 510 U.S. 569 (1994).

- There are some YouTube videos that I choose not to describe here in this respectful and "family-friendly" setting. One, from the show *Family Guy*, uses the Disney classic "When You Wish Upon a Star" as the foundation for a song entitled "I Need a Jew." Such use was determined to be a fair use in the case Bourne Co. v. Twentieth Century Fox Film Corp., 602 F. Supp. 2d 499 (S.D.N.Y. 2009).

- For even more fair use litigation fodder, check out Brownmark Films v. Comedy Partners, 682 F.3d 687, 693 (7th Cir. 2012), evaluating whether *South Park's* version of the "popular" song "What, What in the Butt" constitutes fair use. Fair use has nothing to do with taste.

You can find a list of some other key fair use cases which make some interesting reading at the end of this Guide.

We strongly advise that you make no assumptions about whether the inclusion of music in any context constitutes fair use. A phone call or consultation with your attorney is a necessity in this area.

QUESTIONS FROM OUR AUDIENCE

Q: I'm a news reporter and I'm about to cover the funeral of a local, famous jazz musician who passed away. I understand that musician's music will be played at the funeral. Can that music be a part of my news story without concern about copyright infringement? Would the answer be the same if I was reporting from our local 4th of July parade?

A: Yes, and yes. So long as that music is in the repertory of one of the PROs with which you have a license, your PRO licenses cover the performances of that music. And this sort of use of music may also fall into the category of fair use, especially in the context of coverage of the musician's funeral.

Q: My local television station would like to produce and televise a special program (not a regular newscast) covering my city's annual high school marching band competition. The bands' performances will be front and center. What steps do I need to take to make sure I have all necessary rights in the music performed during the event?

A: If the broadcast is a purely live broadcast and will not be recorded for later viewing, then all the station needs are the necessary public performance rights licenses available from the PROs. If you have licenses from all of the PROs, you are almost certainly covered. If the program is going to be recorded for later viewing, then in addition to securing the necessary public performance rights licenses, you likely also need to secure synchronization rights from music publishers. This will require identifying each musical work included in the performance, and obtaining the necessary synchronization rights.

SECTION 16

"HOT" ISSUES

There are points of debate that have lingered on for years, and some that arise as the ways that consumers listen to music evolve.

You might not encounter the following issues unless you work in the music business. Some have been partially resolved, and some have not. All affect music consumers in one way or another and continue to be fiercely debated.

FRACTIONAL LICENSING

Fractional licenses from a performance rights organization (PRO) convey rights to only the portions of compositions owned by the members of a given PRO. This presents problems for music users if a particular work is owned jointly by multiple publishers or songwriters. The music users would need to secure licenses from each (directly or through their affiliated PRO), unless all the owners belong to the same PRO.

The debate over fractional licensing began when ASCAP and BMI requested that their consent decrees be modified to explicitly allow them to license "fractional" shares of compositions. This request stems from the U.S. Department of Justice's (DOJ's) 2014-2016 review of the PROs' consent decrees described in Section 14.

The DOJ declined to modify the decrees. It concluded that the decrees require the PROs to license on a full-works basis and amending the decrees to allow for fractional licensing would undermine the very rationale for allowing collective licensing in the first place.

BMI promptly challenged the DOJ's interpretation in the federal court with supervisory authority over its decree. The PRO sought a determination that the decree neither prohibits fractional licensing nor requires full-works licensing. The district court agreed with BMI.

The DOJ appealed that determination to the Court of Appeals for the Second Circuit. In late 2017, the appellate court issued a summary order affirming the district court's decision.

Even though the decision concerned only the BMI decree, ASCAP has taken the position that the decision applies equally to its own decree. Notably, the decision only spoke to whether the decree explicitly prohibits fractional licensing, concluding that it does not. The court left open whether allowing fractional licensing would raise competitive concerns.

As a result of these decisions, music users face more significant risks. They cannot rely, for example, on an ASCAP license to grant all the rights necessary to perform all the works in ASCAP's repertory.

For any joint works, the music user needs to be sure that it has a license covering all partial shares, including those controlled by non-ASCAP-affiliated composers and publishers. As a practical matter, this can mean that music users need to have licenses from all PROs to ensure that they are better protected against copyright infringement claims.

INCONSISTENT RATE-SETTING STANDARDS AND JUDICIAL BODIES

As previously noted, different rules govern several different copyright holder rights. Different judicial and administrative bodies decide disputes, and rates are set under different standards.

Certain mechanical reproductions of musical works are the subject of statutory licenses, with rates decided by the Copyright Royalty Board (CRB). Under the new Music Modernization Act, that board will use the "willing buyer/willing seller" standard in setting royalty rates and terms. In other words, the standard calls for setting the rate that a willing buyer and willing seller would agree to in an arm's length transaction in a competitive market. Prior to the passage of the MMA, a different rate-setting standard was used by the CRB.

The CRB also sets rates and terms for the sound recording rights needed by noninteractive streaming services.

Some of the musical works public performance licenses needed by music users can be set by rate courts in Federal District Court in the Southern District of New York. Rate courts use a "reasonable" fee standard—one that calls for the rate that would be set in a competitive market.

Often, of course, music licensing is handled by voluntary, commercial license transactions. As we have discussed, interactive streaming services rely on confidential agreements with record labels to secure all necessary sound recording rights. TV stations negotiate deals for synchronization rights to produce TV content with companies like Universal Production Music, formerly known as Killer Tracks, which produces and licenses music for use in various forms of media.

There are other inconsistencies such as in sound recording fee obligations between digital streaming services and local broadcast radio. Over the air radio broadcasters are not obligated to compensate sound recording owners for the public performance of their recordings. However, they are obligated to pay musical works' owners for performances.

In contrast, digital music services must pay both sound recording owners and musical work owners for performance rights.

PUBLISHER WITHDRAWALS

For decades, publishers have relied on the PROs to license all their public performance rights. But over the last decade, publishers have been trying to selectively withdraw certain rights, such as the right to license digital streaming services, from ASCAP and BMI. In other words, they would like to have the PROs license some users but prevent them from licensing others. Publishers believe that without the middlemen, they and their members would receive higher royalties from this subset of licensees.

Selective withdrawals would allow publishers to negotiate separate (and presumably more lucrative) licensing deals with the big digital music services, such as Spotify. If such withdrawals were allowed, royalties flowing through the PROs might dramatically decrease (depending on the extent of the selective withdrawal by publishers).

The PROs have stated that this would affect their ability to service small publishers. But ASCAP and BMI would also lose some significant sources of revenue. The PROs would be left to negotiate deals with the more cumbersome and labor-intensive music users like bars, restaurants, and entertainment venues, while the publishers would be directly negotiating with some of the largest music users and without the restrictions imposed by the consent decrees.

The rate courts addressed this issue in two separate cases involving Pandora, which were decided in 2013. Both cases reached the same general conclusion: the two consent decrees do not permit selective withdrawal by publishers. However, the courts used different reasoning to reach their decisions.

The ASCAP rate court concluded that when a work is in the repertory for some users, it is in it for all. The BMI court, on the other hand, concluded that if a work is out for some users, it is out for all.

As a result of these rulings, the major publishers put their selective withdrawal efforts on hold. Instead, they began to lobby for either amendments to the consent decrees to allow for selective withdrawals or a legislative solution.

During DOJ's latest review of the consent decrees, the publishers once again expressed their desire to revise the decrees to allow selective withdrawals. Licensees are concerned that partial withdrawals would undermine the protections of the consent decrees and enable publishers to raise rates through the exercise of unfettered market power. There would exist yet another needed music clearance and more fees to pay.

NEW PROS

As new PROs have entered the market, broadcasters and other music users have raised concerns. From the music user perspective, the new PROs increase transaction costs and raise prices, but they don't provide any benefits.

In the last decade, we have seen the growth of SESAC and the entrance of GMR into this space. But there are others and will be more.

The challenge for broadcasters and other music consumers is simple. Getting public performance licenses from ASCAP and BMI is not enough. Public performance rights for many musical works are owned in whole or part by thousands of composers or songwriters not affiliated with ASCAP or BMI. Some of the composers and songwriters might be affiliated with new PROs that aren't widely known. If music users perform any of that music, they are at risk for copyright infringement even if they have valid licenses from ASCAP and BMI.

This problem is compounded by the "fractional licensing" issue described above. The problem is particularly acute for local TV broadcasters that use syndicated programming embedded with music that can't be changed. And the broadcasters do not always know the owner of the music or the PRO representing the copyright holder.

NEED FOR A PUBLIC UNIVERSAL DATABASE

This issue is so critical to local broadcasters and the general music user community at large that the entire next section is devoted to it. Please read on.

SECTION 17

THE FUTURE: CREATION OF A PUBLIC, UNIVERSAL DATABASE

The development of a public, universal database for musical works is a critical step that must be taken.

SUMMARY

The world of music licensing has no public, universal data source. There is no single place to look if you want to identify a song, accurately identify its current and past rightsholders or their PRO affiliations and determine in what media the song has been used.

Currently, ASCAP and BMI have some of this information and make some (but not all) available publicly. Other sources like the rights administration platform owned by Music Reports Inc. have some of this information, but that data is not made publicly available. Even the U.S. Copyright Office does not maintain a complete or near-complete database.

The good news is that a database for musical works' mechanical rights is under development, although it remains to be seen how comprehensive it will be. This was prompted by the Music Modernization Act, described in Section 11. However, there is no database for musical works' public performance rights, the focus of this section.

This is something about which I'm passionate. Because I have a very strong view about the critical need for this type of database, in addition to providing purely factual information, I have also included some commentary.

While a music licensing database has eluded us for decades, it's now a high priority for the broadcast industry. We need to continue advocating for a solution that benefits both music creators and music consumers.

WHAT'S THE PROBLEM?

People know exactly what they are buying or renting in most commercial transactions, for example, exact quantities and item descriptions. This is not true of music licensing. Each of the four PROs offers different blanket licenses covering the musical works in their respective catalogs. Due to a lack of transparency, it's almost impossible to figure out exactly what you are buying.

The available PRO databases are neither comprehensive nor user-friendly. For example, they are not practical for broadcasters that receive syndicated programming with "music in the can." It is certainly not practical for bars and restaurants with slim margins and little time to search a database for each song played by live artists or recorded music played in their venues.

Importantly, affiliation of a songwriter or publisher with a PRO is a bit of a moving target. When they change PRO affiliations, there is no public notice of these decisions. In fact, some of the databases clearly state that users cannot rely on the information they contain to make licensing decisions.

Let's look at the issue in practical terms. What happens if you own a bar or restaurant, and BMI offers to license its music to you? Great idea, right? Your bar will just play "BMI" music and no other music.

Unfortunately, if you did this, your bar or restaurant could be violating the copyright laws.

Even if you limited the songs that are played to just those with a BMI composer, it is probable that these works are not all works solely written by BMI-affiliated songwriters and composers. You might play a song written by several composers (affiliated with different PROs). Or perhaps there is a song with a musical composer affiliated with BMI and a lyricist with GMR. Well, guess what? As a result of fractional licensing, your BMI license may not grant you all the rights necessary to perform these works.

You might need to get licenses from GMR and probably ASCAP and SESAC, unless you can be sure that every musical work you plan to play is fully licensed just through BMI. And, of course, you might play a work that you thought was written by a BMI composer, but it turns out that the composer has switched to a different PRO. The PRO that represents a composer or publisher when a work is first published is not necessarily the same one that represents them 10 years later.

LOCAL BROADCASTERS' ISSUES

When TV and radio outlets negotiate public performance licenses with the PROs, this lack of transparency makes it difficult to determine what constitutes a reasonable fee. It seems logical that payments to an individual PRO should be based, in part, on its market share. For example, if ASCAP accounts for 60% of the music played on local radio stations, shouldn't the local radio industry pay ASCAP 60% of the license fees paid to all PROs for public performance licenses?

The problem is, there is no definitive source that all stakeholders recognize that indicates how much of any PRO music is broadcast in any particular medium.

To get around this problem, TVMLC analyzes music use data to ascertain how much music is being performed on local television, the market shares of each PRO, and how the number of performances and market shares have changed over time. However, these data points are often hotly contested by each PRO, in large part because there is not a single comprehensive publicly available database that has all the information necessary for the analysis and that all stakeholders agree should be used.

Each PRO also maintains its own dataset of the music in local television programming (sometimes called a cue sheet database). These databases have information on what musical works are embedded in which programs; how long the music is played in the program; who the rightsholders are; and each rightsholder's PRO affiliation.

But because the PROs have created databases for the purposes of distributing royalties to their affiliates, they are far more likely to include information about their own affiliates' music than music represented by other PROs. This leads to disagreements between the PROs about their respective shares of local TV performances.

The end result is that if you add up the market share that each PRO claims, the result is well above 100%.

To get a "PRO neutral" assessment of many of these issues, the TVMLC commissions the music use studies discussed in Section 9 under the guidance of economists to ensure that the methodology is statistically valid. The Committee can never fully reconcile its surveys with the cue sheet databases of the PROs without complete access to all the PRO data.

In this era of "big data," it is hard to believe that we can't even agree on what music is played on local TV; who controls it; and how things have changed over time.

Because of these and other similar problems, license negotiations are protracted and costly for the local broadcast industry (and others). Ultimately, stations and the TVMLC want to pay each PRO based on its accurate share of an appropriately sized "total pie" of all public performances on local TV. While the appropriate size of the "pie" might not be agreed to, if there were a comprehensive database that all parties recognized, how the "pie" gets split should be something that everyone can agree on.

AVOIDING FUTURE PROBLEMS

Data transparency has become an increasingly important issue due to three factors:

- The emergence of more unregulated PROs (GMR, Pro Music Rights);
- Fractional licensing;
- Renewed requests from major publishers for the ability to "partially withdraw" from PROs.

It may no longer be enough for stations to have licenses from ASCAP, BMI, and SESAC to ensure they are protected from claims of copyright infringement. The only way to know with certainty that a station is not exposed to copyright infringement lawsuits is to know all the music that is broadcast and whether that music is completely covered by the licenses the station has.

This is an impossibility, given that a lot of music contained in programming and commercials is not identified. What's more, there is no source that stations can definitively rely upon to ascertain what music is covered by their licenses and what is not.

If there was a complete and usable database, with all the information described above, a station could (at least in some instances) determine whether, for example, it needs a license from a new PRO. Alternatively, it would have the information necessary to determine if it can avoid a new PRO's music if that PRO demands an exorbitant fee for its license, if avoidance of the music at issue is possible.

Data transparency will also help minimize per program administration costs. And it should help to promote more direct and source licensing. Knowing exactly what is being licensed through each PRO and what is in each program will help stations figure out where there may be additional opportunities for direct and source licensing.

A NEW PLAN

The ideal database should be comprehensive, downloadable, and fully searchable (without any limitations). All PROs should fully support and back it to avoid any disagreement. The database should also come with appropriate representations and warranties regarding its accuracy, with appropriate indemnifications so that music users can rely upon it.

For audiovisual program providers, two separate databases need to be created:

- A repertory database should contain all musical works with their associated composers; publishers; other rightsholders (including ownership shares); all PRO affiliations (and any caveats to PRO affiliations); all codes (ISWC, etc.); all associated sound recordings with sound recording ownership information and artists; and information about whether any PRO can license the work on a full-works basis.

- A cue sheet database including music in all audiovisual programs and advertisements is critical. And it should be comprehensive. For each program, the database should contain the program title; program episode; all program and episode codes; title of each work (and codes); duration of each work; all owners of each work; the share of each work held by each owner; the PRO affiliation of each owner; and information about whether there are any caveats attached to the PRO affiliation (for example, because of licenses in effect).

With both of these databases in place, TV stations would be able to access essential information concerning what is needed to "clear" a program for the per program license. They could also determine which rightsholders should be approached about direct/source licensing for both the per program license and the adjustable fee blanket license.

Such databases may eliminate disputes regarding the underlying data that helps interested parties to determine how much music is used in local TV programming; which PRO controls what share; and what licenses are required before a program can be broadcast. There still may be disagreements about how the data should be used to arrive at a reasonable fee, but the disputes over what data to use should be eliminated.

The creation of these two databases would require support from not just ASCAP and BMI, but SESAC, GMR, and any other PRO that emerges (e.g., Pro Music Rights).

Note that the databases would not only be useful to local TV. They would provide the same benefits to all audiovisual program providers (for example, Netflix, cable channels, and YouTube).

HOW TO MOVE FORWARD

Despite this era of big data, there still is no publicly available comprehensive database that identifies what music is included in TV programming and who controls the music. An authoritative database would reduce inefficiencies; provide clarity for music owners and music consumers; and help to promote fair, accurate, and reasonable payment for music based on audience and usage.

FUTURE LEGISLATION

As the U.S. Congress continues its review of the copyright laws governing music licensing, TVMLC and other members of the MIC Coalition are hopeful that reforms are advanced, achieving a healthy balance in the new music economy. This includes the creation of a modern music copyright database, as described above, that would provide a transparent, accurate, and fully searchable record of music ownership and licensing information available to everyone.

This would result in more efficient licensing and payment accuracy. This up-to-date information should be available to the public in an easily accessible format. In the current non-transparent system, music users do not even know precisely what they are licensing from each PRO.

If you are interested in learning more about the work of the MIC Coalition to create more transparency in music licensing, please visit their website at www.mic-coalition.org.

AFTERWORD

How songwriters and artists distribute music and how audiences receive and listen to music has changed dramatically over the last decade and continues to change. CDs have gone the way of records. Interactive streaming has eclipsed digital downloads as the primary means that consumers access music and "singles" will eclipse "albums."

With the digital age, there is an increased reliance on performance royalties as compared to reproduction and distribution royalties. As broadcast media evolves and audience flocks to new sources of entertainment, the music creators and their representatives will see fewer dollars flowing in from broadcast TV and radio and more dollars from Netflix, Amazon Music, Apple, YouTube and other new media.

Despite the rapid change in how music is delivered, certain challenges and principles remain constant. In 2015, the U.S. Copyright Office in its Music Marketplace Study listed as a resource below developed the following **Guiding Principles.** While we do not agree with all of them, the following makes universal sense to music users -

1. Music creators should be fairly compensated.
2. The licensing process should be more efficient.
3. Market participants should have access to authoritative data to identify and license sound recordings and musical works.
4. Usage and payment information should be transparent and accessible to copyright owners.
5. Government licensing processes should aspire to treat like uses of music alike.

6. Government supervision should enable voluntary transactions while still supporting collective solutions.
7. Rate setting and enforcement of antitrust laws should be separately managed and addressed.
8. A single, market-oriented rate setting standard should apply to all music uses under statutory licenses.
9. Both copyright owners and music services must be able to uniquely identify particular sound recordings and underlying musical works, along with the dynamic and often fractured ownership status of these distinct works. In addition, they need to be able to pair sound recordings with the musical works they embody. While the industry has made some progress on this front, much remains to be done.

> The bottom line is the more transparency, the better.

The bottom line is the more transparency, the better. There is not universal agreement on who controls what. The lack of a public, universal, complete, real-time accessible database is a major stumbling block to a more efficient and competitive marketplace.

ADDITIONAL READING – FAIR USE – SECTION 15

Here is a list of some other key fair use cases which make some interesting reading:

- Hustler Magazine, Inc. v. Moral Majority, Inc., 606 F. Supp. 1526 (C.D. Cal. 1985)
- Wright v. Warner Books, Inc., 953 F.2d 731 (2d Cir. 1991)
- Cambridge University Press v. Patton, 769 F.3d 1232 (11th Cir. Ga. 2014)
- The Author's Guild v. Hathitrust, 755 F.3d 87 (2d Cir. 2014)
- Swatch Grp. Mgmt. Servs. Ltd. v. Bloomberg L.P., 742 F.3d 17 (2d Cir. 2014)
- TCA Television Corp. v. McCollum, No. 15 Civ. 4325 (S.D.N.Y. Dec. 17, 2015)
- Harper & Row v. Nation Enters., 471 U.S. 539 (1985)
- Salinger v. Random House, 811 F.2d 90 (2d Cir. 1987)
- Love v. Kwitny, 772 F. Supp. 1367 (S.D.N.Y., 1989)
- Twin Peaks v. Publications Int'l, Ltd., 996 F.2d 1366 (2d Cir. 1993)
- Castle Rock Entertainment, Inc. v. Carol Publ. Group, 150 F.3d 132 (2d Cir. 1998)
- Salinger v. Colting, 641 F. Supp. 2d 250 (S.D.N.Y. 2009)
- Warner Bros. Entertainment, Inc. v. RDR Books, 575 F. Supp. 2d 513 (S.D.N.Y. 2008)
- Universal City Studios v. Sony Corp., 464 U.S. 417 (1984)

- Monster Communications, Inc. v. Turner Broadcasting Sys. Inc., 935 F. Supp. 490 (S.D.N.Y., 1996)
- Kelly v. Arriba-Soft, 336 F.3d 811 (9th Cir. 2003)
- Bill Graham Archives v. Dorling Kindersley Ltd., 448 F.3d 605 (2d Cir. 2006)
- Perfect 10, Inc. v. Amazon.com, Inc., 508 F.3d 1146 (9th Cir. 2007)
- Warren Publishing Co. v. Spurlock, 645 F. Supp. 2d 402 (E.D. Pa. 2009)
- SOFA Entertainment, Inc. v. Dodger Productions, Inc., No. 2:08-cv-02616 (9th Cir. Mar. 11, 2013)
- Arrow Productions, Ltd., v. The Weinstein Company, LLC, 2014 WL 4211350 (S.D.N.Y. Aug. 25, 2014)
- Kienitz v. Sconnie Nation LLC, 766 F.3d 756 (7th Cir. 2014)
- Fox News v. TVEYES, Inc., 43 F. Supp. 3d 379 (S.D.N.Y. 2014)
- Equals Three, LLC v. Jukin Media, Inc., 14-09041 (C.D. Cal. Oct. 13, 2015)
- Los Angeles News Service v. KCAL-TV Channel 9, 108 F.3d 1119 (9th Cir. 1997)
- Ringgold v. Black Entertainment Television, Inc., 126 F.3d 70 (2d Cir. 1997)
- Authors Guild v. Google, Inc., No. 13-4829 (2d Cir. 2015)

RESOURCES

For further information, particularly with respect to the business, legislative and judicial history of music licensing, I refer you to the following –

"Kohn on Music Licensing" -
   https://www.bobkohn.com/kohn-on-music-licensing

"Copyright and the Music Marketplace Study"—A Report of the Register of Copyrights—February 2015
   https://www.copyright.gov/policy/musiclicensingstudy/copyright-and-the-music-marketplace.pdf

RIGHTS BY MEDIA TYPE – MUSICAL WORKS

MEDIA TYPE	PERFORMANCE RIGHTS	REPRODUCTION & RELATED RIGHTS
Local Television	Secured from PROs or directly from rightsholders	Synch rights: typically secured from publishers or music libraries
Network Television	Secured from PROs or directly from rightsholders	Synch rights: typically secured from publishers or music libraries
Cable Television	Secured from PROs or directly from rightsholders	Synch rights: typically secured from publishers or music libraries
Audio-Visual Streaming Services (i.e., Netflix)	Secured from PROs or directly from rightsholders	Synch rights: typically secured from publishers or music libraries
Broadcast Radio	Secured from PROs or directly from rightsholders	Not Needed
Satellite Radio	Secured from PROs or directly from rightsholders	Not Needed
Simulcast Streams Of Broadcast Radio	Secured from PROs or directly from rightsholders	Not Needed
Interactive Streaming (i.e., Spotify)	Secured from PROs or directly from rightsholders	Section 115 Statutory License (Mechanical Rights)
Non-interactive Streaming (i.e., Pandora's Main Service)	Secured from PROs or directly from rightsholders	Not Needed
Digital Download Stores	Not Needed	Section 115 Statutory License (Mechanical Rights)
Live Music Venues (Bars, Restaurants, Concert Venues)	Secured from PROs or directly from rightsholders	Not Needed

RIGHTS BY MEDIA TYPE – SOUND RECORDINGS

MEDIA TYPE	PERFORMANCE RIGHTS	REPRODUCTION & RELATED RIGHTS
Local Television	Not Needed	Master Use Rights: typically secured from record labels or music libraries
Network Television	Not Needed	Master Use Rights: typically secured from record labels or music libraries
Cable Television	Not Needed	Master Use Rights: typically secured from record labels or music libraries
Audio-Visual Streaming Services (i.e., Netflix)	Not Needed	Master Use Rights: typically secured from record labels or music libraries
Broadcast Radio	Not Needed	Not Needed
Satellite Radio	Section 114 Statutory License	Section 112 Statutory License (ephemeral recordings)
Simulcast Streams Of Broadcast Radio	Section 114 Statutory License	Section 112 Statutory License (ephemeral recordings)
Interactive Streaming (i.e., Spotify)	Directly from Record Labels and other rightsholders	Directly from Record Labels and other rightsholders
Non-interactive Streaming (i.e., Pandora's Main Service)	Section 114 Statutory License	Section 112 Statutory License (ephemeral recordings)
Digital Download Stores	Not Needed	Directly from Record Labels and other rightsholders
Live Music Venues (Bars, Restaurants, Concert Venues)	Not Needed	Not Needed

www.ingramcontent.com/pod-product-compliance
Lightning Source LLC
Chambersburg PA
CBHW061737070526
44585CB00024B/2712